# SIGNING
# MADE EASY

A COMPLETE PROGRAM FOR LEARNING SIGN LANGUAGE.
INCLUDES SENTENCE DRILLS AND EXERCISES FOR INCREASED
COMPREHENSION AND SIGNING SKILL.

## ROD R. BUTTERWORTH, M.A., M.Ed.,
## AND MICKEY FLODIN

A PERIGEE BOOK

*To Joanna,*
*my ever faithful companion in life.*
*R.R.B.*


*To my best friend*
*and greatest source of encouragement,*
*my loving wife, Carol.*
*M.F.*

A Perigee Book
published by
The Berkley Publishing Group
A division of Penguin Putnam Inc.
375 Hudson Street
New York, New York 10014

The Penguin Putnam Inc. World Wide Web site address is
http://www.penguinputnam.com

Library of Congress Cataloging-in-Publication Data

Butterworth, Rod. R.
Signing made easy : a complete program for learning sign language,
includes sentence drills and exercises for increased comprehension
and signing skill / Rod R. Butterworth and Mickey Flodin.
          p.    cm.
Includes index.
ISBN 0-399-51490-2
1. Sign Language—Study and teaching.  2. Sign language—Problems,
exercises, etc.  I. Flodin, Mickey.  II. Title.
HV2474.B88      1989        88-23878 CIP
419′.07–dc19

Cover design by Dale Fiorillo
Cover photography by Alexa Garbarino

Printed in the United States of America

33   32

# Acknowledgments

We wish to thank the following for their expertise, help, and encouragement in completing *Signing Made Easy*. As in most projects of this nature, the amount of work and details needing attention turned out to be more than expected, but with willing assistance from key people, the job was made much easier and enjoyable. Therefore, we wish to thank:

Karen R. Twigg, who has had a wide range of experience in her almost twenty years of teaching and interpreting sign language. Her special abilities have earned her notable recognition as a leader in the deaf community. She has studied interpreting skills at Akron University, Akron, Ohio; has taught sign language at Baptist Bible College, Springfield, Missouri; and earned her B.A. and M.S. in science at Southwest Missouri State University, Springfield, Missouri. In addition, she has taught interpreters' classes and has been able to apply interpreting skills in schools, courtrooms, hospitals, and churches. Her current goal is to establish interpreters' seminars across the country. For *Signing Made Easy* she has offered valuable suggestions and hints that have contributed to the overall smoothness and accuracy of the final text.

Joanna Butterworth, for careful proofreading and determination to complete the seemingly endless task of alphabetizing descriptions for each page.

Winifred Butterworth, for her patience and willingness to proofread the first draft.

Carol Flodin, who painstakingly number-coded each page of the text of almost 4,000 signs, and who provided delicious meals and snacks and words of encouragement on those long Saturday afternoons.

Daniel Flodin, who alphabetized all the original artwork, and who once again waited patiently for his dad to finish writing a book.

Roger Scholl, senior editor, Perigee Books, for his belief, inspiration, and guidance throughout this project.

Nancy Peske, editorial assistant, Perigee Books, for her many hours of editing, numerous and invaluable suggestions, and fine tuning of the manuscript.

Terri Letterman, for cutting and pasting up the descriptions used from *The Perigee Visual Dictionary of Signing*.

R.R.B.
M.F.

# Contents

# Foreword

In my nearly twenty years of teaching sign language and working with hearing-impaired people, I have never seen another sign language book comparable to *Signing Made Easy*. The authors have developed a variety of creative ideas and combined them into one very inclusive text. The book is unique in its total approach.

One ingredient missing in other sign language books is a way to practice reverse signing skills (looking at the sign and recognizing its meaning). Each chapter of this book gives a review of signs by themselves, and the student has to provide the English equivalent. These receptive skills are more difficult to grasp than the expressive skills, and are often neglected by teachers of sign language as well as available texts.

As a teacher of sign language to people of all ages, individually, in church classes, public schools, colleges, and so on, I've been anxiously awaiting a sign language text—more than just a book of signs. *Signing Made Easy* is a text that will meet the needs of the individual trying to learn sign language on his own, and the classroom teacher of sign language who needs to give tests and quizzes to determine a grade.

When I teach sign language I stress that *repetition is the key* to learning and that *if you don't use it, you will lose it!* This text provides opportunities for repetition through the great variety found in its presentation and review sections. Using it with consistent practice will lead the student onward to proficiency in sign language.

Karen R. Twigg
M.S. Secondary Education
Certified deaf/hearing-impaired teacher

# Introduction

*Signing Made Easy* has been designed to do just that, to make learning sign language easier. It features unique sections for the student to practice *receiving* as well as learning and giving signs. To our knowledge, this is the first book of its kind that offers such a complete learning system.

The one area that is lacking in many of the existing sign language books is that of material to teach and aid the student in receiving signs. This is always one of the more challenging and difficult aspects of learning sign language, but in *Signing Made Easy* the student is immediately given the opportunity to practice the art of receptive skills at his own rate.

In the Practice Learning Signs sections the student will benefit from clear illustrations given in English syntax for learning the signs within a conversational context. Also provided are concise and accurate descriptions for all the signs used in this book. Any description that cannot be found on the page where the word occurs can be found by looking it up in the index. However, most words are described on the page on which they appear, especially if it is the first instance of a word's usage in the book.

The Practice Giving Signs sections in every chapter reinforce learning by repeating the previous sentences from the Practice Learning Signs sections, but without the illustrations. This challenges the student to recall what he has just studied and learned.

To further the learning process a variety of exercises are provided within each chapter. These include Test Your Skill: Matching, Multiple Choice, Fill In the Blanks, Fingerspelling, Vocabulary Review, and Extra Practice. Each of these exercises utilizes material from the current or previous chapters. By this method the student not only benefits once again from the application of the law of repetition but also gains by learning to adapt to diversity of expression—thus helping him develop flexibility in his signing. For example, the Fill In the Blanks sections require the student to choose appropriate signs from those he has already learned in order to complete the sentence logically.

Developing proficiency in sign language takes time and practice, but even after the first lesson or two of *Signing Made Easy,* the student will be able to communicate with simple vocabulary and concepts. After completing this book one can continue to expand his vocabulary through the use of the authors' previously published work *The Perigee Visual Dictionary of Signing.*

Just as the English language constantly evolves, so does the sign language of the deaf. New signs are often created within the deaf community, and sometimes spread across the country until they become generally accepted. The signs used in this book are commonly used and accepted in the North American continent, but within various geographical communities of the deaf one will often find slight differences and preferences concerning the way to make a particular sign.

Sign language is a living language that is becoming increasingly popular across the nation. In addition to its natural practical usage for communication, more and more people are discovering sign language as an art form for use in music, theaters, and churches.

The authors believe that everyone who studies diligently with *Signing Made Easy* will find it to be both an enjoyable experience and a book that lives up to its name.

# History

It was in the sixteenth century that Geronimo Cardano, a physician, of Padua, in northern Italy, proclaimed that the deaf could be taught to understand written combinations of symbols by associating them with the thing they represented. The first book on teaching sign language to the deaf that contained the manual alphabet was published in 1620 by Juan Pablo de Bonet.

In 1755 Abbé Charles Michel de L'Epée of Paris founded the first free school for the deaf. He taught that the deaf could develop communication with themselves and the hearing world through a system of conventional gestures, hand signs, and fingerspelling. He created and demonstrated a language of signs whereby each sign would be a symbol that suggested the concept desired.

The abbé was apparently a very creative person, and the way he developed his sign language system was by first recognizing then learning the signs that were *already being used* by a group of deaf people in Paris. To this knowledge he added his own creativeness which resulted in a signed version of spoken French. He paved the way for the deaf to have a more standardized language of their own—one which would effectively bridge the gap between the hearing and nonhearing worlds.

Another prominent deaf educator of the same period (1778) was Samuel Heinicke of Leipzig, Germany. Heinicke did not use the manual method of communication but taught speech and speechreading. He established the first public school for the deaf that achieved government recognition. These two methods (manual and oral) were the forerunners of today's concept of total communication. Total communication espouses the use of all means of available communication such as sign language, gesturing, fingerspelling, speechreading, speech, use of hearing aids, reading, writing, and pictures.

In America the Great Plains Indians had developed a fairly extensive system of signing, but this was more for intertribal communication than for the deaf, and only vestiges of it remain today. However, it is interesting to note some similarities existing between Indian sign language and the present system.

America owes a tremendous debt of gratitude to Thomas Hopkins Gallaudet, an energetic Congregational minister who became interested in helping his neighbor's young deaf daughter, Alice Cogswell. He traveled to Europe in 1815, when he was twenty-seven, to study methods of communicating with the deaf. While in England he met Abbé Roche Ambroise Sicard, who invited him to study at his school for the deaf in Paris. After several months he returned to the United States with Laurent Clerc, a deaf sign language instructor from the Paris school.

In 1817 Gallaudet founded the first school for the deaf in Hartford, Connecticut, and Clerc became the first United States deaf sign language teacher. Soon schools for the deaf began to appear in several states. Among them was the New York School for the Deaf, which opened its doors in 1818. In 1820 a school was opened in Pennsylvania, and a total of twenty-two schools had been established throughout the United States by the year 1863.

An important milestone in the history of deaf education was the founding of Gallaudet College, in Washington, D.C., in 1864, which remains the only liberal arts college for the deaf in the United States and the world.

Thomas Hopkins Gallaudet passed on his dream of a college for the deaf to his son, Edward Miner Gallaudet, who with the help of Amos Kendall made the dream a reality. Edward Miner Gallaudet became the first president of the new college.

Today we are fortunate to have one of the most complete and expressive sign language systems of any country in the world. We owe much to the French sign system, from which many of our present-day signs, though modified, have been derived.

It might be noted here that many deaf people use a special grammatical structure when signing, usually among themselves, known technically as American Sign Language, or ASL. But signing in English word order continues to grow in popularity and is widely used by both the deaf and the hearing. It is easier for a hearing person to learn sign language in English syntax than to learn signing with the grammatical structure of ASL.

Interest continues to grow in sign language, and it is now the fourth most used language in the United States. Many sign language classes are offered in communities, churches, and colleges.

# How to Use This Book

By now you have probably read the introduction and are familiar with some of the unique teaching methods and procedures contained in this book. We encourage you to read all of this section before beginning your journey into the exciting world of sign language.

Each chapter begins with a section titled Practice Learning Signs. Read the sentences out loud and sign each word simultaneously. Be sure to read and study the descriptions given at the bottom of the page to ensure accuracy. Look in the index for descriptions not provided on that particular page. Notice that many words have synonyms which can also be expressed through the same basic sign. The sentences are not designed to tell a particular story, but relate only to the general subject area of the chapter.

You will notice words enclosed in slashes (/) in a number of the sentences. For example, /perfect/. In addition, at the end of most Practice Learning Signs sections, several extra words are contained within slashes. All these words within slash marks are alternatives for increased vocabulary, flexibility, and variety of expression.

Once you feel satisfied you have learned the signs sufficiently and are reasonably comfortable in using them, proceed to the Practice Giving Signs section. Now, without referring back to the Practice Learning Signs section, sign the sentences by trying to recall the signs you have just studied. Cover the opposite page with a sheet of paper before commencing. Evaluate your progress and repeat any sentences in which you feel there is a need for improvement.

Next, we want to work on developing your receptive skills; one of the unique aspects of this book is that it will enable you to study receiving signs on your own. As you look at the first page of Practice Receiving Signs, imagine that someone is signing to you. If a sign has one or more arrows indicating movement, try to visualize that movement. Say the words out loud if circumstances permit. Once again, do not move on to the next section until you are sure you have learned the material thoroughly.

## MANUAL ALPHABET AND FINGERSPELLING

It is absolutely essential that the manual alphabet is mastered at the outset of learning sign language.

This is not very difficult and you will probably be spelling out words slowly in an hour or two. Speed comes with practice, but remember that most people prefer a reasonable rate for fingerspelling because of the amount of concentration needed to receive and understand it. When receiving fingerspelling learn to read words as groups of letters rather than individual letters.

Fingerspelling is used mainly for names of people, places, and words for which there are no formal signs, or for when the formal sign has not been learned. You will notice that some of the manual alphabet hand shapes resemble the configuration of English letters.

When fingerspelling, hold your hand in a comfortable position slightly above shoulder level with the palm facing forward. There is no need for jerky exaggerated hand or arm movements. Strive to combine the letters smoothly and at a comfortable speed. When spelling words with double letters, such as *will,* move the *L* hand slightly to the right to sign the second letter *L*.

Each chapter contains a fingerspelling exercise. We strongly urge you to practice each exercise two or three times as you progress through the book. These exercises will help you develop dexterity and rhythm. By the time you reach Chapter 12 you may be able to fingerspell longer and more difficult words such as *Shakespeare* and *Philadelphia* with ease.

## EXERCISES AND QUIZZES

To reinforce the material you have already studied you will find exercises and quizzes included in every chapter. These are: Vocabulary Review, Multiple Choice, Test Your Skill: Matching, Extra Practice, and Fill In the Blanks. Each of these contains vocabulary from the chapter being studied, except for Vocabulary Review, which in most cases is a comprehensive review of material learned thus far. All sections have appropriate instructions. Answers for quizzes are provided on page 217.

## SIGN DIRECTION AND ORIENTATION

The illustrations are drawn as you would see another person signing to you. This is not the same as looking into a mirror, for then the right hand would appear to be the left hand. To make the signs clearer and more easily understood, some illustrations are shown from an angle or profile perspective.

Arrows have been provided in order for the student to comprehend clearly a sign's movement and direction. When a movement is described as clockwise or counterclockwise, it is to be understood from the viewpoint of the signer and not from the viewpoint of the observer.

## INDEX

Words that have been used in the sentences or within slash marks are printed in bold type. Synonyms are printed in lightface type.

# Suggestions and Tips for Easier Signing

## THE SIGNING AREA

Most signs are made in an area extending from head to waist, and shoulder to shoulder. The majority of these signs are formed at or near the head, face, and neck area. This makes it easier for the person receiving the signs to observe and understand them more readily. When you are in between sentences or waiting for a response, hold your hand in a comfortable position at chest level or at your side.

Facial expression is extremely important when signing to the deaf. The deaf person relies heavily upon the combination of facial expressions, body language, and speaking or mouthing the words. Therefore, be sure to include these as you sign.

## DEFINITE AND INDEFINITE ARTICLES

Sometimes signers omit the definite and indefinite articles (*the, a, an*) when by so doing the meaning of the sentence is not altered. Obviously this would speed up the interchange of conversation. However, when young deaf children are being taught English language structure in the classroom setting, all words are signed.

## POSSESSIVES AND PLURALS

As in the case of the definite and indefinite articles, the possessive ('s) and plurals are usually omitted by most signers. But once again, they may be signed for the purpose of conveying exact English syntax. The authors have not deemed it necessary to include the signs for these within the text. This is due to both space limitations and the fact that possessives and plurals are generally understood within context. Furthermore, in practice they are often omitted except in situations where the English language is being taught. You will find the possessive and plural signs under "Inflections" on page 15, if you decide to use them.

## PUNCTUATION

When asking a question either use the question mark sign at the end of a sentence, or make a questioning facial expression and hold the last sign a little longer. Punctuation can be used for exactness and emphasis when needed or desired but is often omitted in favor of facial expressions and gestures.

## GENDER SIGNS

The male and female gender signs are identified more easily by their location. Many male-related signs are made adjacent to the forehead, while the cheek or chin is the location for many female-related signs.

## THE PERSON ENDING

This sign (as described on page 43) usually relates to a person's occupation or position in life. Some examples of its use would be: sign *bake* plus the *person ending* for *baker;* sign *America* plus the *person ending* for *American.*

## SIGNS WITH SIMILAR SHAPES, MOVEMENTS, AND CHARACTERISTICS

There are several factors that help make sign language a little easier to learn and remember. Certain signs have similar shapes and movements, and in some cases signs simply reverse the movement while the hand shapes remain unchanged. For example: *come* and *go; open* and *close;* and *get in* and *get out.*

In addition, some signs resemble or remind one of the actual physical concept they represent. For example: the sign for *elephant* portrays the elephant's trunk, while the sign for *golf* portrays the use of a golf club.

Sometimes recognizing the origin of a sign helps to recall the sign more easily. For example: the sign for *milk* has its origin in the action of milking a cow.

There are also signs that are initialized by using the hand shape of the first letter of the English word. Some examples are: *parents, family,* and *nephew.* Initialization of signs appears to be a growing trend, and one that certainly aids signers and receivers of signs who desire to communicate in English syntax.

## PRESENT, PAST, AND FUTURE

To understand the sign language concept of present, past, and future, the student should think of the area immediately in front of the body as representing *present* time. Therefore, signs dealing with present time are made in front of the body. Signs referring to the future (*tomorrow, next*) have a forward movement away from the body. Signs that deal with the past (*last week, yesterday*) move backward.

# Hand Shapes

This book refers to certain basic hand shapes which are used in the descriptions to aid the student in forming the signs correctly. Familiarize yourself with the following illustrations:

## THE *AND* HAND

Note that unless otherwise stated, the expression refers only to the ending position of the *and* hand as it is here illustrated.

**OPEN HAND**    **CLOSED HAND**

## FLAT HAND

The fingers are touching unless otherwise indicated by the use of a term such as "flat *open* hand."

**BENT HAND**    **CLAWED HAND**

## CURVED HAND

The fingers are touching unless otherwise indicated by the use of a term such as "curved *open* hand."

# Inflections

Following are some of the word endings commonly used. They may be added to the basic signs for more exact expression when appropriate.

**-MENT**

**-NESS**

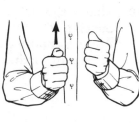

**-ER**

**-EST**

**-ING**

**-'S**

**-S**

**-ED**
Sign *past.*

**-ED**
(Alternative)

**-EN**

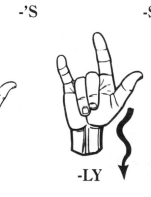

**-Y**

**-LY**

**-LY**
Sign *L;* then *Y.*
(Alternative)

# Numbers

The palm generally faces forward unless otherwise indicated by illustration or description. Sign numbers, money, and years as they are spoken in English. For example: $57.35 is signed "57" "dollar" "35" "cents"; and 1988 is signed "19" "88."

ZERO TO A MILLION

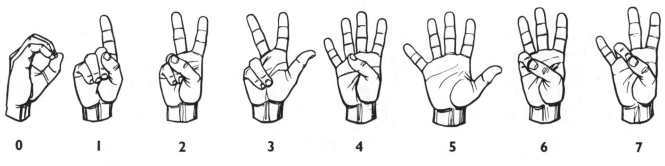

| 0 | I | 2 | 3 | 4 | 5 | 6 | 7 |

**8**        **9**        **10**  Shake the extended A-hand thumb back and forth.

**11**  Flick the index finger up with palm facing self.

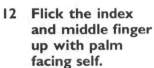

**12**  Flick the index and middle finger up with palm facing self.

**13**  Move the fingers of the 3 hand up and down with palm facing self.

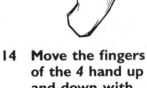

**14**  Move the fingers of the 4 hand up and down with palm facing self.

**15**  Move the fingers of the 5 hand up and down with palm facing self.

**16**  Sign *10*, then 6.

**17**  Sign *10*, then 7.

**18**  Sign *10*, then 8.

**19**  Sign *10*, then 9.

**20**

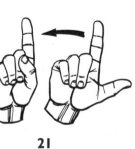

**21**

**22**

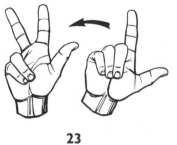

**23**

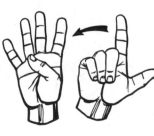

**24**

**25**

**26**

 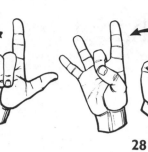 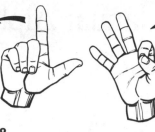 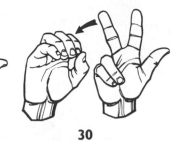

| 27 | 28 | 29 | 30 |

## HUNDRED

Sign *I* (*one*), then *C*.

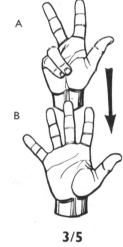

## THOUSAND

Bring the right *M* fingertips down into the flat left hand.

## MILLION

Bring the right *M* fingertips down into the flat left palm twice.

## FRACTIONS

Sign the upper half of the fraction first, then lower the hand a short distance and sign the lower half.

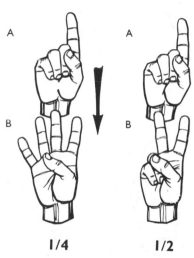

| 1/4 | 1/2 | 3/5 |

## CENTS

| 1¢ | 8¢ |

## DOLLARS

A quick way for signing *dollars* 1 to 9 is with the palm facing forward, then dipping downward slightly as it turns until the palm faces self.

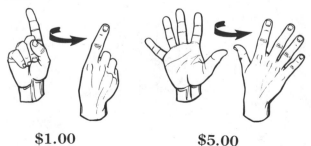

| $1.00 | $5.00 |

## NUMBERS FOR PRACTICE

| 7 | 179 | 657 | 6,112 |
| 10 | 276 | 741 | 7,499 |
| 17 | 286 | 827 | 7,673 |
| 19 | 292 | 903 | 7,725 |
| 22 | 295 | 1,431 | 7,817 |
| 31 | 306 | 2,702 | 8,888 |
| 47 | 420 | 3,258 | 9,852 |
| 58 | 576 | 4,946 | 10,146 |
| 69 | 602 | 5,328 | 11,539 |
| 72 | 610 | 5,577 | 1,219,803 |
| 85 | 621 | 5,693 | 39,462,971 |
| 94 | 644 | 6,549 | 968,359,712 |

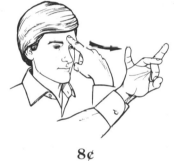

# The Manual Alphabet

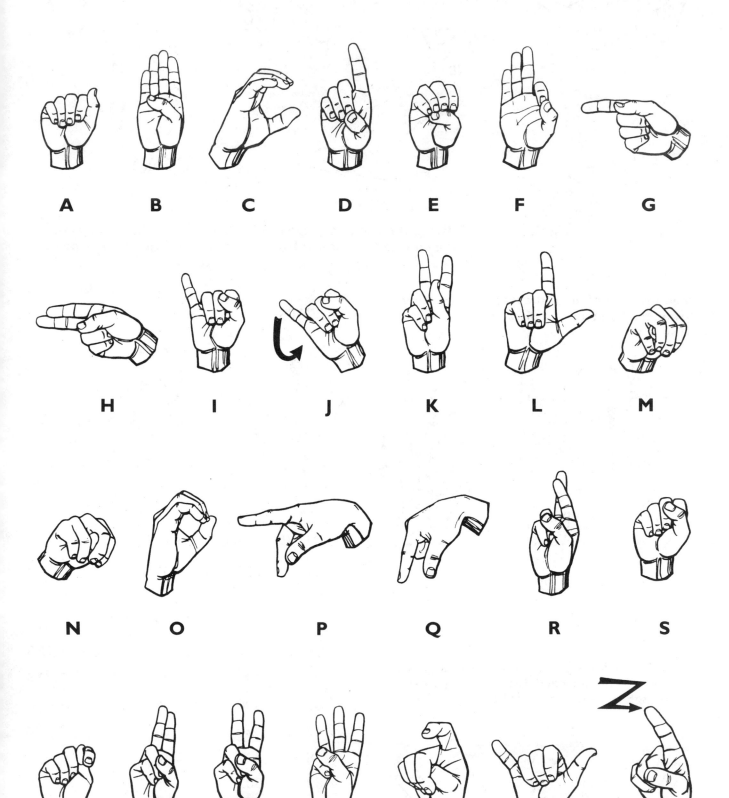

# Family
# and
# Social Life

# Practice Learning Signs

Learn and practice the signs and sentences on each page before proceeding to the next. Descriptions are supplied at the bottom of each page.

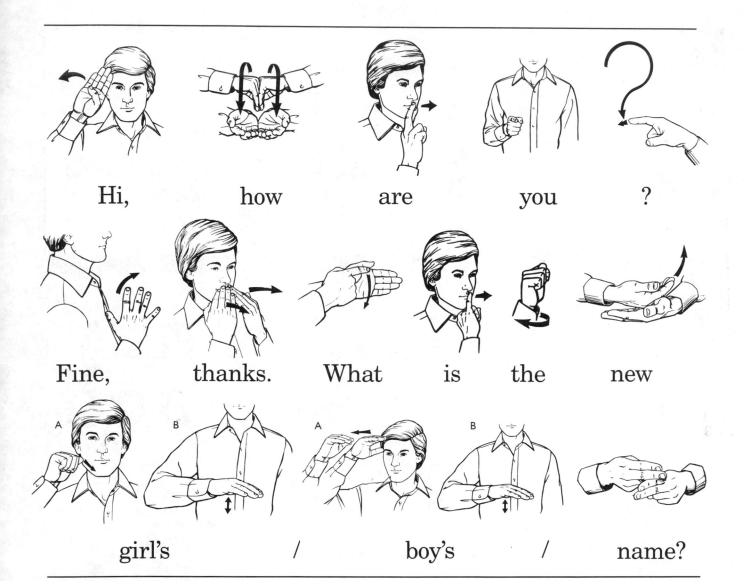

Hi,     how     are     you     ?

Fine,     thanks.     What     is     the     new

girl's     /     boy's     /     name?

**ARE, AM, BE, IS:** For *are,* move right *R* fingers forward from the mouth. For *am* use *A,* for *be* use *B,* for *is* use *I.*

**BOY:** First sign *male:* Move the right hand to forehead as if gripping the bill of a cap, move the hand forward a short distance; then move the right flat palm-down hand to waist level to indicate the height of a boy. *Note:* Some omit the latter movement.

**FINE:** Place the thumb edge of the right flat open hand at the chest and pivot the hand forward.

**GIRL:** First sign *female:* Trace the right jawbone from ear to chin with the palm side of the right *A* thumb; then move the right flat hand to waist level with palm facing down to indicate the height of a girl. *Note:* Some omit the latter movement.

**HOW:** Point the fingers of both bent hands down and place hands back to back. Revolve hands in and upward together until palms are flat and facing up.

**NAME, CALLED, NAMED:** Cross the middle-finger edge of the right *H* fingers over the index-finger edge of the left *H* fingers. To sign *called* or *named,* move crossed *H* hands in a small forward arc together.

**NEW:** Pass the back of the right slightly curved hand across the left flat palm from fingers to heel. Continue movement of the right hand in a slight upward direction.

**QUESTION:** Draw a small question mark in the air. *Note: For the remainder of this book, the sign for question is neither illustrated nor described, to conserve space.*

**THANKS, THANK YOU, YOU'RE WELCOME:** Move both flat hands forward and down from the lips until palms face upward.

**THE:** Rotate the right *T* hand counterclockwise.

**WHAT:** Pass the tip of the right index finger down over the left flat hand from the index to the little finger.

LOOK IN INDEX FOR LOCATION OF ADDITIONAL DESCRIPTIONS.

20

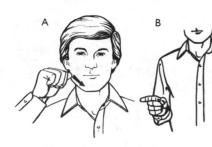  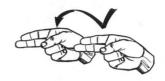 

**She**      **is**      **hard-of-hearing.**      **Yes.**

**No.**      **Sign**      **slowly.**      **Respect**      **/ obey /**

**your**      **parents.**      **Mother's**      **expression**      **was**

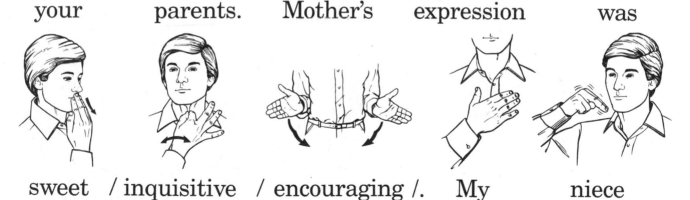

**sweet / inquisitive / encouraging /.**      **My**      **niece**

---

**ENCOURAGE, MOTIVATE:** Move both flat (or open) hands forward with several short dipping movements.

**EXPRESSION:** Move both *X* (or modified *A*) hands up and down alternately at the sides of the face.

**HARD-OF-HEARING:** Point the right *H* hand forward and move it in a short arc to the right.

**INQUISITIVE, CURIOUS:** Pinch the neck and wiggle the hand slightly.

**MOTHER:** Touch the chin with the thumb of the right open hand.

**NIECE:** Shake *N*-hand fingers near the chin.

**NO:** Bring the right thumb and the index and middle fingers together.

**OBEY, OBEDIENCE:** Move both *S* hands down and forward while changing them to palm-up flat hands.

**PARENTS:** Place the middle finger of the right *P* hand at the right temple, then at the right side of the chin.

**SHE, HER:** First sign *female;* then point the index finger forward. If it is obvious that a female is being referred to, the sign for *female* can be omitted.

**SIGNS (DEAF LANGUAGE):** Hold both index fingers to the front with the fingers pointing toward each other and the palms facing out. Rotate both index fingers alternately toward the body.

**SLOW:** Draw the right-hand fingertips slowly up the back of the left hand.

**WAS:** Move the right *W* hand back to the cheek while changing it to an *S* hand.

**YES:** Nod the right *S* hand up and down with palm facing forward.

**YOUR, HIS, HER, THEIR:** Push the right flat hand forward with palm facing the person referred to. The signs for *male* and *female* can precede *his* and *her* if it is not obvious from the context. Add a final move to the right for *your* in the plural.

LOOK IN INDEX FOR LOCATION OF ADDITIONAL DESCRIPTIONS.

and    nephew    also    visited    Grandma.

Our    sister's    wedding    was    beautiful

/perfect/.    Clean    your    room    and

make    your    bed.    Where    is

**ALSO, TOO:** Bring both index fingers together with the palms facing down. Repeat slightly to the left.

**BEAUTIFUL, ATTRACTIVE, HANDSOME, LOVELY, PRETTY:** Place the fingertips of the right *and* hand at the chin and open the hand as it describes a counterclockwise circle around the face. The *H* hand can be used when signing *handsome.*

**CLEAN, NICE, PURE:** Move the palm of the right flat hand across the palm of the left flat hand from wrist to fingertips.

**GRANDMOTHER:** Touch the chin with the thumb of the right open hand which has its palm facing left. Move the right hand in two forward arcs.

**MAKE, FASHION, FIX:** Strike the right *S* hand on the top of the left *S* hand and twist the hands slightly inward. Repeat for emphasis as needed.

**NEPHEW:** Place the right extended *N* fingers close to the right temple and shake back and forth from the wrist.

**OUR:** Place the slightly cupped right hand on the right side of the chest with palm facing left. Move the right hand forward in a circular motion, bringing it to rest near the left shoulder with the palm facing right.

**PERFECT:** Move the middle fingertips of both *P* hands together so that they touch.

**ROOM:** Outline the sides and shape of a square in two movements with both flat hands. *R* hands can be used also.

**SISTER:** First sign *female;* then sign *same:* Point both index fingers forward and bring them together.

**VISIT:** Hold both *V* hands up with palms facing in. Rotate them forward alternately.

**WEDDING:** Point the fingers of both flat hands down from the wrists in the front. Swing the hands toward each other until the left fingers and thumb grasp the right fingers.

**WHERE:** Shake the right index finger from side to side with palm facing forward.

LOOK IN INDEX FOR LOCATION OF ADDITIONAL DESCRIPTIONS.

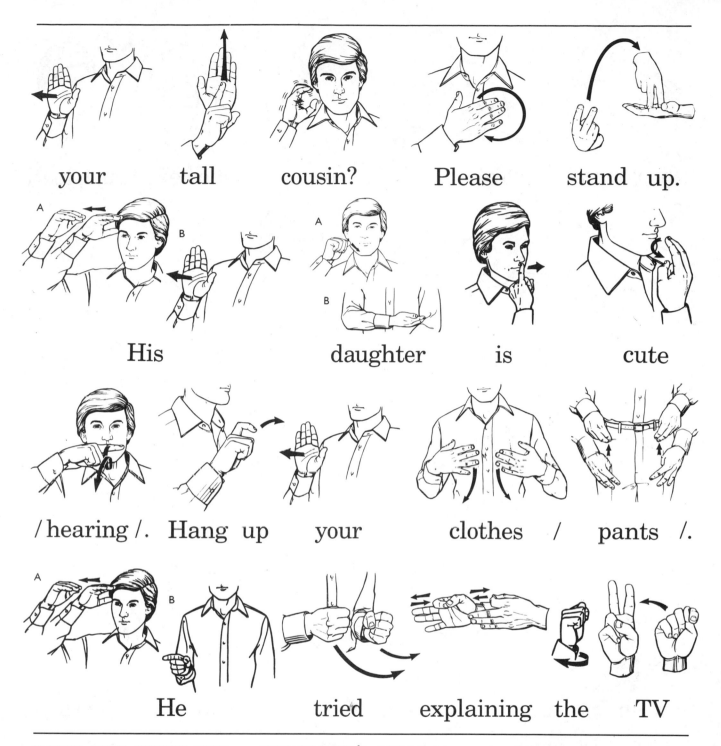

your   tall   cousin?   Please   stand up.

His   daughter   is   cute

/ hearing /. Hang up   your   clothes / pants /.

He   tried   explaining   the   TV

**CLOTHES, DRESS, GARMENT, GOWN, SUIT, WEAR:** Brush the fingertips of both flat open hands down the chest a few times.

**COUSIN:** Place the right C hand either close to the right temple for a male or close to the right cheek for a female; then shake back and forth from the wrist.

**CUTE:** Stroke the chin several times with the fingers of the right U hand. Assume a smiling expression.

**DAUGHTER:** First sign *female,* then move the right flat hand with palm facing up into the crook of the left bent elbow.

**EXPLAIN, DEFINE, DESCRIBE:** Move both F (or D) hands back and forth alternately with palms facing.

**HANG UP, HANGER, SUSPEND:** With palm facing forward, move the right X hand up and forward a short distance. *Alternative:* Hang the right X finger on the left index finger, which is pointing to the right.

**HEARING:** Place the right index finger in front of the mouth and make a few small forward circular movements.

**PANTS, SLACKS, TROUSERS:** Place the curved open hands just below the waist and move them up to the waist while simultaneously forming *and* hands.

**PLEASE, ENJOY, GRATIFY, LIKE, PLEASURE:** Make a counterclockwise circle with the right flat hand over the heart.

**STAND UP, ARISE, GET UP:** Begin with the right V fingers pointing up and the palm facing in. Make an arc with the V fingers until they rest in an upright position on the left upturned palm.

**TALL:** Place the right index finger on the left flat palm and move it straight up.

**TRY, ATTEMPT, EFFORT:** Hold both S (or T) hands in front with palms facing, then push hands forward. For *attempt* use A hands, for *effort* use E hands.

LOOK IN INDEX FOR LOCATION OF ADDITIONAL DESCRIPTIONS.

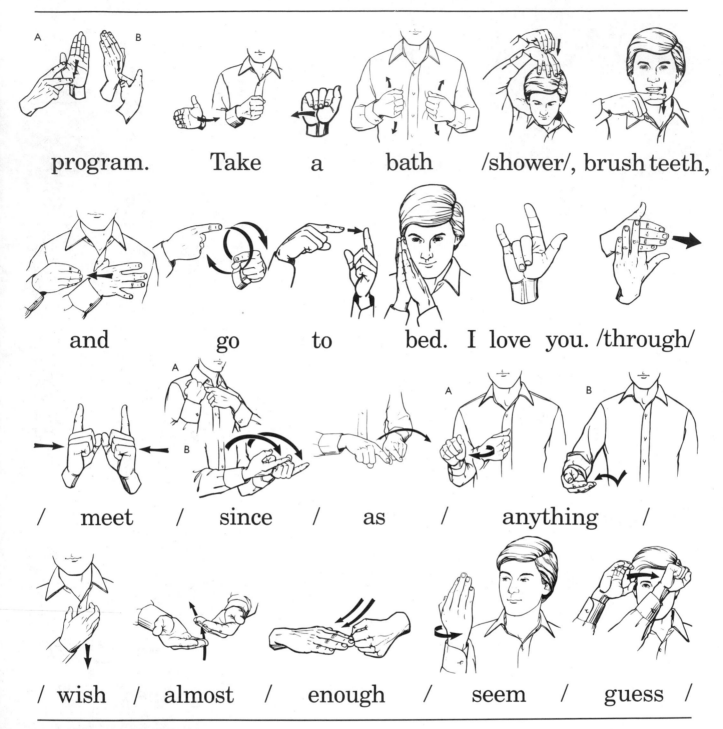

program. Take a bath /shower/, brush teeth,

and go to bed. I love you. /through/

/ meet / since / as / anything /

/ wish / almost / enough / seem / guess /

**ALMOST, NEARLY:** Brush the little-finger edge of the right hand upward over the fingertips of the curved left hand. Both palms face up.

**ANYTHING, THING, SUBSTANCE:** Swing the right *A* hand forward and to the right. Then drop the right flat palm-up hand a few times while moving it to the right.

**AS:** Point both index fingers forward together with a short distance between them and the palms facing down. Maintain this position as both hands are moved to the left.

**BATH, BATHE:** Rub both *A* hands up and down on the chest several times.

**BRUSH (YOUR) TEETH, TOOTHBRUSH:** Shake the right horizontal index finger up and down in front of the teeth.

**ENOUGH, PLENTY, SUFFICIENT:** Move the right flat hand across the top of the left *S* hand a few times.

**GO:** Point both index fingers toward each other and rotate them around each other as they are moved away from the body.

**I LOVE YOU:** Hold the right hand up with palm facing forward. The thumb and the index and little fingers are extended.

**PROGRAM:** Move the middle finger of the right *P* hand down the left flat palm; then down the back of the left hand.

**SHOWER, BAPTIZE, CHRISTEN:** Place the closed *S* (or *and*) hand above the head and thrust downward toward the head while simultaneously opening the hand.

**TAKE:** Place the right open hand forward and draw it into the chest while simultaneously forming a closed hand.

**THROUGH, VIA:** Pass the little-finger edge of the right flat hand forward between the left index and middle fingers.

**WISH:** With the palm facing in, draw the right *C* hand down the chest from just below the neck.

LOOK IN INDEX FOR LOCATION OF ADDITIONAL DESCRIPTIONS.

# Practice Giving Signs

Practice signing the following sentences once again. Try to do so without referring back to the illustrations. You can also cover the page opposite if you wish.

Hi, how are you? Fine, thanks.

What is the new girl's /boy's/ name?

She is hard-of-hearing.

Yes. No. Sign slowly.

Respect /obey/ your parents.

Mother's expression was sweet /inquisitive/ encouraging/.

My niece and nephew also visited Grandma.

Our sister's wedding was beautiful /perfect/.

Clean your room and make your bed.

Where is your tall cousin?

Please stand up.

His daughter is cute /hearing/.

Hang up your clothes /pants/.

He tried explaining the TV program.

Take a bath /shower/, brush (your) teeth, and go to bed.

I love you.

/through/meet/since/as/anything/wish/almost/ enough/seem/guess/

# Fingerspelling Practice

Practice the following words at least twice with a speed that is both steady and comfortable for you. See "How to Use This Book" on page 12 for more instructions.

| on | to | by | vet | mud | Tom |
|----|----|----|-----|-----|-----|
| go | up | if | van | toe | zoo |
| at | by | hi | car | but | new |
| do | be | it | kit | rat | pen |
| an | as | we | hot | let | big |
| so | or | no | hit | saw | Pam |
| in | am | he | sun | dip | old |

# Practice Receiving Signs

Interpret the following signs. Practicing by this method will help you receive and understand signs more easily. Say the words out loud as you proceed.

Never    forget    family    responsibilities.

Open / close / the    door / window / again.

The    kids    were    punished    by    Father.

She    refused / promised /

**AGAIN, ENCORE, REPEAT:** Place the right bent hand fingertips into the left palm.
**DOOR:** Hold both *B* hands to the front with palms facing out and index fingers touching. Twist the right hand back and forth from the wrist.
**FAMILY:** Place both upright *F* hands to the front with the palms facing each other. Make an outward circular movement with each hand simultaneously until the little fingers touch.
**FATHER:** Touch the forehead with the right open-hand thumb.
**FORGET, FORSAKE:** Wipe the palm side of the right open hand across the forehead from left to right. End with the right hand in

the *A* position close to the right temple.
**KID (CHILD):** With index and little finger extended, pivot the right hand up and down as it moves left across the upper lip.
**NEVER:** Trace a half-circle in the air to the right with the right flat hand; then drop the hand away to the right.
**PROMISE:** Touch the lips with the right index finger; then move the right flat hand down and slap it against the thumb and index-finger side of the closed left hand.
**PUNISH:** Strike the right index finger along the underside of the left forearm to the elbow.
**REFUSE, WON'T:** Hold the right *S* (or *A*) hand in a natural position to the front; then

move it sharply upward over the right shoulder while simultaneously turning the head to the left.
**RESPONSIBILITY, BURDEN, OBLIGATION:** Place the fingers of both curved hands on the right shoulder. Sometimes both *R* hands are placed on the right shoulder to sign *responsibility*.
**WINDOW:** Place the little-finger edge of the right flat hand on the thumb edge of the left flat hand with palms facing in. Move the right hand up a short distance.

LOOK IN INDEX FOR LOCATION OF ADDITIONAL DESCRIPTIONS.

to      share      the      secret.      Your      husband's

gift      was      something      special.

The      gentleman      smiled      and      asked

for      a      dance.      Choose      a      chair      to

**ASK, REQUEST:** Bring both flat hands together with palms touching and move them in a backward arc toward the body.

**CHAIR:** Place the palm side of the right *H* fingers on the back of the left *H* fingers.

**DANCE, BALL:** Point the left flat upturned hand to the right; then swing the downturned fingers of the right *V* hand from side to side over the left palm.

**GENTLEMAN:** First sign *male;* then sign *fine.*

**GIFT, AWARD, BESTOW, CONFER, CONTRIBUTE, PRESENT, REWARD:** With palms facing each other, place both closed hands to the front with the thumb tips touching the inside of their respective crooked index fingers. Move both hands forward simultaneously in an arc.

**HUSBAND:** First sign *male;* then sign *marriage:* Clasp hands with the right hand above the left.

**SHARE:** Move the little-finger edge of the right flat hand back and forth on the left flat hand between the fingers and wrist.

**SMILE, GRIN:** Stroke the cheeks backward and upward with the fingers of both hands.

**SOMETHING:** First sign *some:* Place the right curved hand on the left palm; pull the right hand toward self while forming it into a flat hand. Then sign *thing.*

**SPECIAL, EXCEPT, EXCEPTIONAL, EXTRAORDINARY, OUTSTANDING, UNIQUE:** Point the left index finger up and take hold of it with the right thumb and index finger. Raise both hands together.

LOOK IN INDEX FOR LOCATION OF ADDITIONAL DESCRIPTIONS.

sit       on.       I       never       imagined

the       woman's       marriage       would       end

in       divorce.       I       find       it

easier       to       wash dishes       myself.       Wash

---

**DIVORCE:** Touch *D* hands together; then move them apart.

**EASY, SIMPLE:** Hold the left curved hand to the front with the palm up. Brush the little-finger edge of the right curved hand upward over the fingertips of the left hand several times.

**END, COMPLETE, CONCLUDE, DONE, FINISH:** Hold the left flat hand with fingers pointing forward and palm facing right. Move the fingers of the right flat hand outward along the index-finger edge of the left until it drops off the end.

**FIND, DISCOVER:** Hold the right open hand in front with the palm facing down. Bring the index and thumb together as the hand is raised.

**IMAGINATION, FICTION, THEORY:** Hold the right *I* hand near the forehead with palm facing in. Move the *I* hand forward and up-ward in a few rolling circles. *Note:* To sign *fiction,* use an *F* hand, and to sign *theory,* use a *T* hand.

**IN, INTO, ENTER:** Move the closed fingers of the right hand into the left *C* hand. *Note:* To sign *into* and *enter,* the right fingers can be pushed down right through the left *C* hand.

**MARRIAGE:** Clasp the hands in a natural position with the right hand above the left.

**MYSELF, SELF:** Bring the *A* hand against the center of the chest with palm facing left.

**ON:** With both palms facing down, place the right flat hand on the back of the left flat hand.

**SIT, BE SEATED, SEAT:** First sign *chair;* then move both hands down slightly.

**WASH:** Rub the knuckles of both closed hands together with circular movements.

**WOMAN:** Touch the thumb of the right open hand on the chin, then on the chest.

**WOULD:** Move the right *W* hand forward while changing it to a *D* hand.

LOOK IN INDEX FOR LOCATION OF ADDITIONAL DESCRIPTIONS.

the  dirty  kitchen  floor  with  soap.

I'm  awake  and

can't  sleep.  Don't  tease.  My

wife  introduced  her  bachelor

---

**AWAKE, AROUSE, WAKE UP:** Place the closed thumbs and index fingers of both *Q* hands at the corners of the eyes; then open eyes and fingers simultaneously.

**BACHELOR:** Put the index finger of the right *B* hand first on the right side of the mouth, then on the left. Some reverse this action.

**CAN'T, CANNOT, IMPOSSIBLE, INCAPABLE, UNABLE:** Strike the left index finger with the right index finger as it makes a downward movement. The left index maintains its position.

**DO NOT, NOT:** Place the right *A* thumb under the chin and move it forward and away from the chin.

**FLOOR:** Place the index-finger edge of both flat hands together with palms facing down; then move both hands apart to the sides.

**INTRODUCE:** Move both flat hands in from the sides with palms up until the fingertips almost touch.

**SLEEP, DOZE, NAP, SIESTA, SLUMBER:** Place the palm side of the right open hand in front of the face and move it down to chin level while forming an *and* hand.

**SOAP:** Brush the right fingertips across the left palm several times. *Note:* Variations in the direction and manner of rubbing exist for this sign.

**TEASE, DAMAGE, PERSECUTE, RUIN,**

**SPOIL, TORMENT:** Hold both closed hands to the front with both thumb tips in the crook of their respective index fingers. Move the knuckles of the right hand forward across the top of the left hand. Repeat according to emphasis required.

**WIFE:** First sign *female;* then clasp the hands in a natural position with the right hand above the left. The latter is the sign for *marriage.*

**WITH, WITHOUT:** To sign *with,* join the two *A* hands with palms facing. To sign *without,* begin with the same basic position; then separate the hands and move them outward while simultaneously forming open hands.

---

LOOK IN INDEX FOR LOCATION OF ADDITIONAL DESCRIPTIONS.

brother / to / the / neighbor. / Aunt

and / Uncle / are / coming. / /voice

up / down / all right / another / engaged
(prior to marriage)

/ wide / drop / blanket / mean (verb) / rest /

**ALL RIGHT, OK:** Hold the left flat hand with palm facing up. Move the little-finger edge of the right flat hand across the face of the left hand from the heel to the fingertips. *OK* is often fingerspelled.

**ANOTHER, OTHER:** Hold the right *A* hand in front of the chest with upturned thumb. Pivot the hand from the wrist so that the thumb points to the right.

**AUNT:** Place the right *A* hand close to the right cheek and shake back and forth from the wrist.

**BROTHER:** First sign *male;* then, sign *same:* With one movement, point both index fingers forward and bring them together.

**COME:** Point both index fingers toward each other and rotate them around each other while simultaneously moving them toward the body.

**DROP:** Drop both *S* hands while simultaneously changing to open hands.

**ENGAGED (PRIOR TO MARRIAGE):** Circle the right *E* hand over the left palm-down flat hand; then place the right *E* on the left ring finger.

**MEAN (VERB), INTEND, PURPOSE:** Place the fingertips of the right *V* hand in the palm of the left flat hand, which has its palm facing either to the right or upward. Draw the right hand away slightly; rotate it in a

clockwise direction and rethrust the *V* fingers into the left palm.

**NEIGHBOR:** Hold the left curved hand away from the body with palm facing in. Move the back of the right curved hand close to the palm of the left. Bring both flat hands down simultaneously with palms facing each other. This is a combination of *near* and *person* (personalizing word ending).

**UNCLE:** With the palm facing forward, place the right *U* hand close to the right temple and shake back and forth from the wrist.

**VOICE, VOCAL:** Draw the back of the right *V* fingers up the neck and forward under the chin.

LOOK IN INDEX FOR LOCATION OF ADDITIONAL DESCRIPTIONS.

# Practice Giving Signs

Practice signing the following sentences once again. Try to do so without referring back to the illustrations. You can also cover the page opposite if you wish.

Never forget family responsibilities.

Open /close/ the door /window/ again.

The kids were punished by Father.

She refused /promised/ to share the secret.

Your husband's gift was something special.

The gentleman smiled and asked for a dance.

Choose a chair to sit on.

I never imagined the woman's marriage would end in divorce.

I find it easier to wash dishes myself.

Wash the dirty kitchen floor with soap.

I'm awake and can't sleep.

Don't tease.

My wife introduced her bachelor brother to the neighbor.

Aunt and Uncle are coming.

/voice/up/down/all right/another/ engaged (prior to marriage)/wide/drop/ blanket/mean (verb)/rest/

# Vocabulary Review

Identify the following signs from this chapter to reinforce your vocabulary.

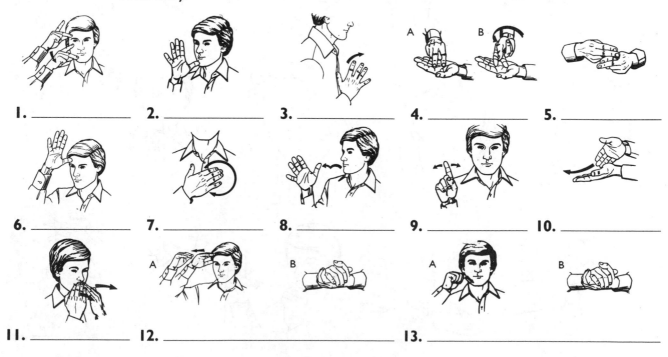

1. _____  2. _____  3. _____  4. _____  5. _____

6. _____  7. _____  8. _____  9. _____  10. _____

11. _____  12. _____  13. _____

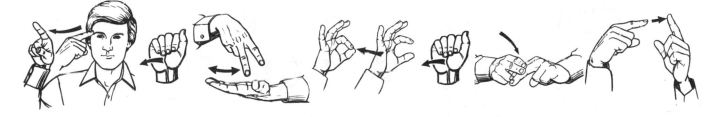

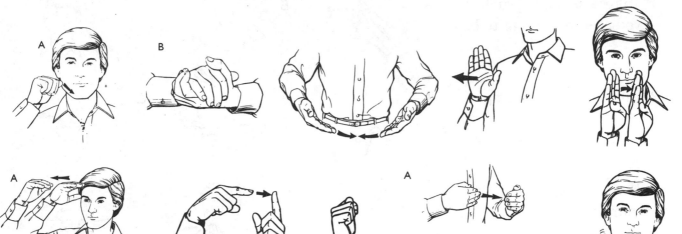
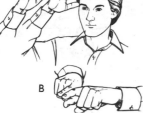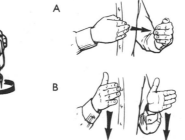
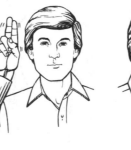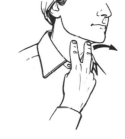
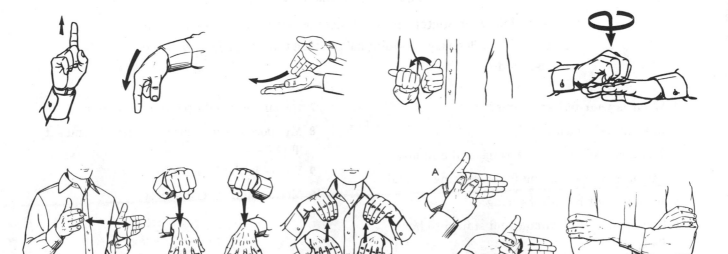

# Multiple Choice

Draw a circle around or place a check mark beside the sign that matches the italicized word. For additional practice you can sign all the words in the sentences.

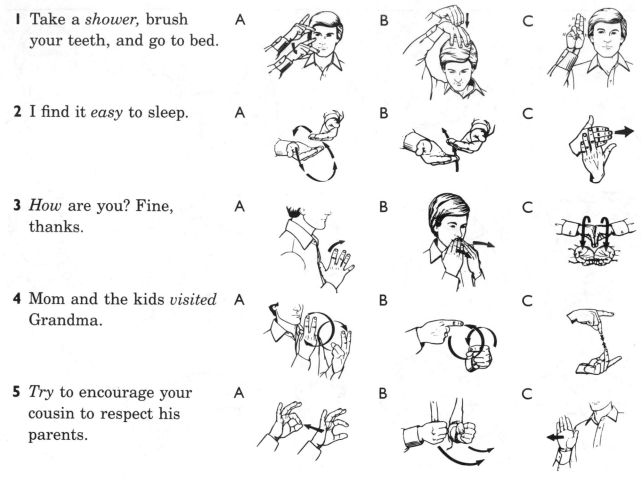

**1** Take a *shower,* brush your teeth, and go to bed.   A   B   C

**2** I find it *easy* to sleep.   A   B   C

**3** *How* are you? Fine, thanks.   A   B   C

**4** Mom and the kids *visited* Grandma.   A   B   C

**5** *Try* to encourage your cousin to respect his parents.   A   B   C

# Extra Practice

Sign the following sentences which contain words chosen from this chapter. This will give you additional practice using the signs you have just learned.

**1** What is your father's name?

**2** Is your room clean?

**3** The girl dreamed of marriage and a family.

**4** The kids were wishing for something special.

**5** Is your aunt hard-of-hearing?

**6** She opened the window and smiled to her neighbor.

**7** I wish you would try to sign slowly.

**8** My niece chose a chair by the TV and sat quietly.

**9** Where is the blanket?

**10** Mother's gift was a secret.

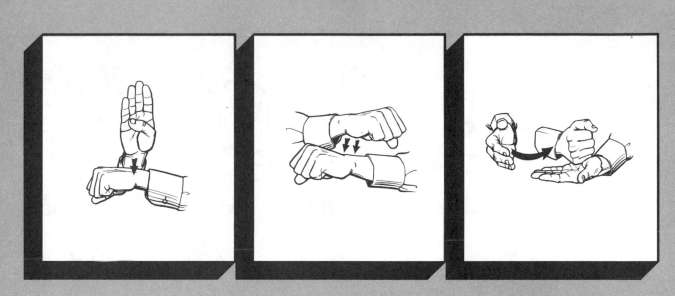

# Work
# and
# Careers

2

# Practice Learning Signs

Learn and practice the signs and sentences on each page before proceeding to the next. Descriptions are supplied at the bottom of each page.

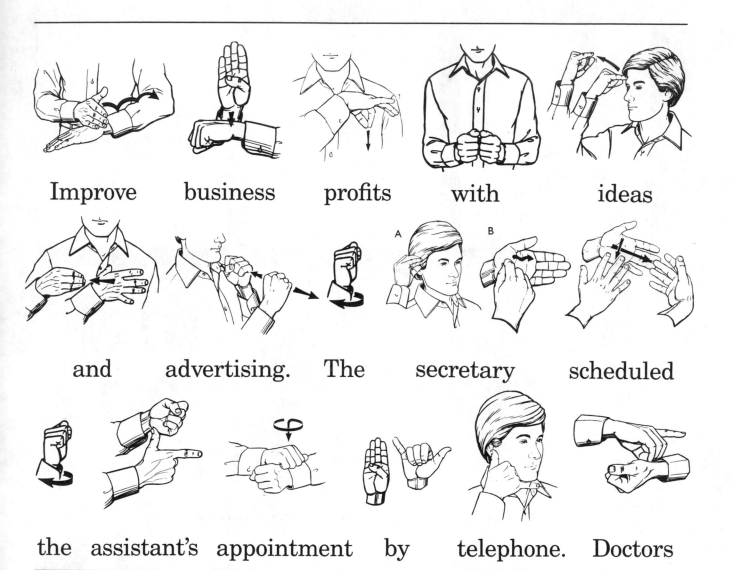

Improve business profits with ideas

and advertising. The secretary scheduled

the assistant's appointment by telephone. Doctors

**ADVERTISE, COMMERCIAL, PUBLICIZE:** Place the left *S* hand in front of the mouth area with the palm facing right and the right *S* hand in front of the left. Move the right *S* hand forward and backward a few times.

**APPOINTMENT, ENGAGEMENT, RESERVATION:** Circle the right palm-down *A* hand above the left palm-in *S* hand in a clockwise direction. Bring the right wrist down onto the left and move both hands down together a short distance.

**ASSISTANT:** Bring the right *L* hand up under the left closed hand and touch the little-finger edge of the left hand with the right thumb. Sometimes the left hand remains open.

**BUSINESS:** Strike the wrist of the right *B* hand on the downturned wrist of the left closed hand a few times. The right *B* hand faces forward.

**DOCTOR, PHYSICIAN, PSYCHIATRY, SURGEON:** Touch the left wrist with the right *D* (or *M*) fingertips. Use a *P* hand for *psychiatry*.

**IDEA, CONCEPT, OPINION:** Move the right *I* finger (or *C* or *O* hand shapes, for *concept* or *opinion*, respectively) forward and up from the forehead.

**IMPROVE:** Move the little-finger edge of the right flat hand in small arcs up the left arm.

**PROFIT, BENEFIT, GAIN:** Place the touching thumb and index finger of the right *F*

hand into an imaginary shirt pocket.

**SCHEDULE:** Hold the left open hand to the front with palm facing right. Move the right open hand down across the left hand with palms facing; then move the back of the right hand across the left hand from left to right.

**SECRETARY:** Remove an imaginary pencil from above the right ear, and mimic handwriting action on the left flat hand.

**TELEPHONE, CALL:** Position the *Y* hand at the right of the face so that the thumb is near the ear and the little finger near the mouth.

**WITH:** Join both *A* hands together.

LOOK IN INDEX FOR LOCATION OF ADDITIONAL DESCRIPTIONS.

and     lawyers     usually     receive

good     salaries.     Tom's     work

is     building     government     housing.     Who

is     your     new     boss?     That

**BOSS, CHAIRMAN, OFFICER:** Touch the right shoulder with the fingertips of the right curved open hand.

**BUILD, CONSTRUCT, ERECT:** Place each hand above the other alternately.

**GOOD, WELL:** Move the right flat hand down from the mouth to rest in the left hand.

**GOVERNMENT, CAPITAL, FEDERAL, POLITICS:** Make a small circle and touch the temple with the right index fingers. Initialize *capital, federal,* and *politics,* and add the sign for *person* (personalizing word ending) when signing *governor.*

**HOUSE, RESIDENCE:** Outline the roof and walls of a house.

**LAWYER, ATTORNEY, LAW:** Place the in-dex and thumb side of the right *L* hand on the front of the left palm-forward hand. Be-gin near the top; then move the right hand downward in a small arc to the base of the left hand. To sign *attorney* and *lawyer,* add the sign for *person* (personalizing word ending).

**PERSON (PERSONALIZING WORD END-ING):** Hold both flat open hands to the front with palms facing; then move them down simultaneously.

**RECEIVE, ACQUIRE, GET, OBTAIN:** Bring both open hands together while simultane-ously forming *S* hands; place right on top of left.

**SALARY, COLLECT, EARN, WAGES:** Sweep the curved right hand across the left palm-up flat hand, and end with the right hand closed.

**THAT:** Place the right downturned *Y* hand on the left upturned palm. *Note:* Omit the sign for *that* when it is a conjunctive, as in the sentence "It is good *that* you trust me."

**USUALLY, USED TO:** Point the fingers of the right *U* hand upward. Place the right wrist on the wrist of the left downturned closed hand; push hands down slightly.

**WHO, WHOM:** Make a counterclockwise circle in front of the lips with the right index.

**WORK, JOB, LABOR, TASK:** With palms down, tap the wrist of the right *S* hand on the wrist of the left *S* hand a few times.

LOOK IN INDEX FOR LOCATION OF ADDITIONAL DESCRIPTIONS.

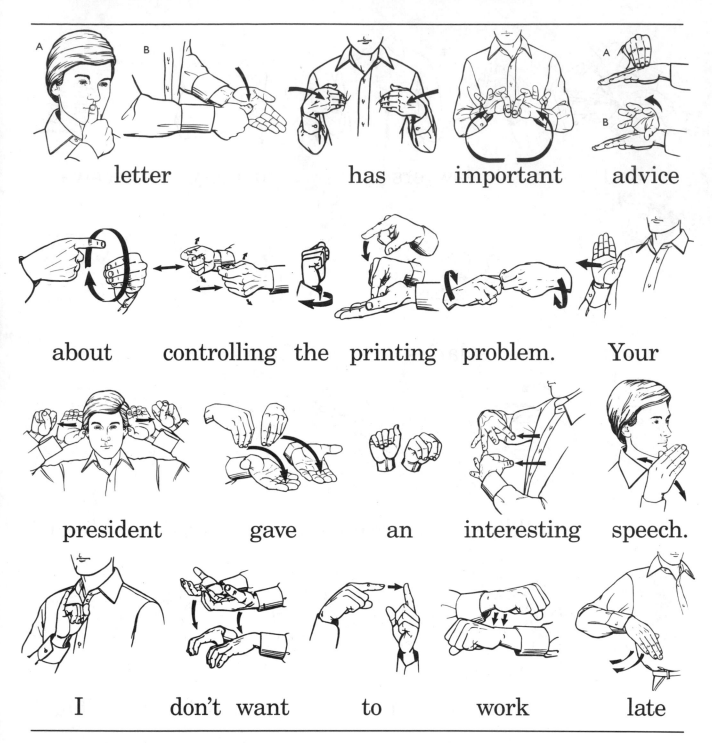

letter ⋅ has ⋅ important ⋅ advice ⋅ about ⋅ controlling ⋅ the ⋅ printing ⋅ problem. ⋅ Your ⋅ president ⋅ gave ⋅ an ⋅ interesting ⋅ speech. ⋅ I ⋅ don't ⋅ want ⋅ to ⋅ work ⋅ late

**ADVICE, ADVISE, COUNSEL:** Touch the back of the left flat hand with the fingertips of the right *and* hand. Open right hand while moving it forward across the left hand.

**CONTROL, DIRECT, GOVERN, MANAGE, OPERATE, REGULATE, REIGN, RULE:** Close both hands with the thumb tips in the crook of the index fingers. Hold both hands parallel; then move them back and forth with a slight pivoting action from the wrists.

**DON'T WANT:** Move both open curved hands from a palm-up to a palm-down position.

**GIVE, DISTRIBUTE:** Hold both *and* hands to the front with palms facing down. Move them forward simultaneously while forming flat hands with fingers pointing forward and palms facing up.

**HAS, HAD, HAVE, OWN, POSSESS:** Place the fingertips of both bent hands on the chest. Some signers use *S* hands for *has, D* hands for *had,* and *V* hands for *have.*

**IMPORTANT, MERIT, PRECIOUS, SIGNIFICANT, USEFUL, VALUABLE, WORTHY:** Bring both *F* hands up to the center of the chest; turn them palms down with thumbs and indexes touching.

**INTEREST:** Place the thumb and index finger of each hand on the chest, with one hand above the other. Bring the index fingers and thumbs together as the hands are moved forward. Keep the other fingers extended.

**LETTER, MAIL:** Place the right *A* thumb on the mouth and then on the palm of the upturned left hand.

**PRESIDENT, SUPERINTENDENT:** Hold both *C* hands at the temples with palms facing forward. Change to the *S* position as the hands are moved upward and outward.

**PRINTING, PUBLISHING, NEWSPAPER:** Move the right index finger and thumb together as though picking something up; then place them on the left flat palm.

**PROBLEM, DIFFICULTY:** Touch the bent knuckles of the two *U* (or *V*) hands together and twist in opposite directions while moving downward slightly.

LOOK IN INDEX FOR LOCATION OF ADDITIONAL DESCRIPTIONS.

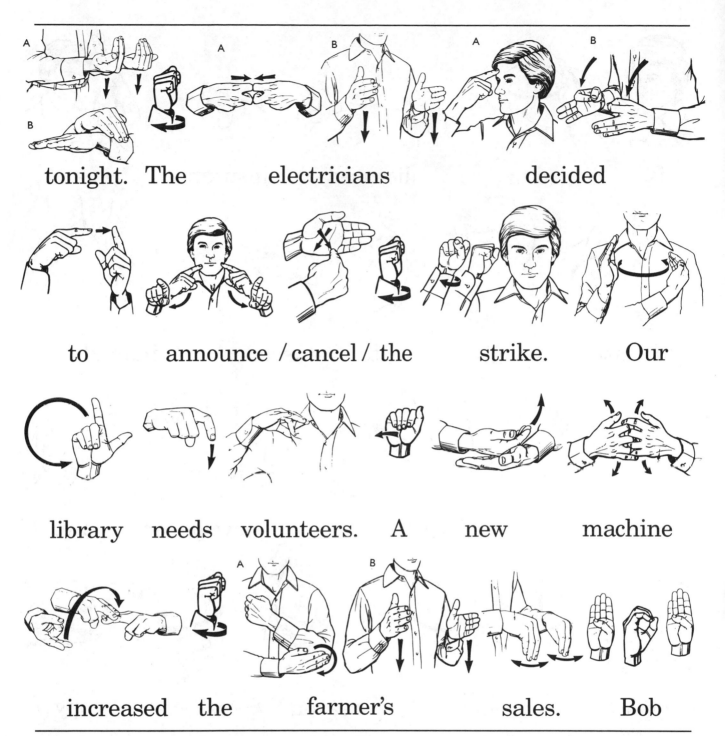

tonight. The electricians decided

to announce / cancel / the strike. Our

library needs volunteers. A new machine

increased the farmer's sales. Bob

**ANNOUNCE, DECLARE, PROCLAIM:** Touch the lips with both index fingers and swing them forward and to the sides.

**DECIDE, DECISION, DETERMINE, MAKE UP ONE'S MIND:** Touch the forehead with the right index finger, then bring both *F* hands down with palms facing.

**ELECTRICITY, PHYSICS:** Strike the bent index and middle fingers of each hand (or just the index fingers) together a few times. The other fingers are closed.

**INCREASE, ADD, GAIN WEIGHT, LOSE WEIGHT:** Move the right *H* fingers from a palm-up position to a palm-down position and place them on the left palm-down *H*

fingers. Repeat a few times. To sign *lose weight,* reverse the action.

**LIBRARY:** Make a small clockwise circle with the right *L* hand.

**MACHINE, ENGINE, FACTORY, MECHANISM, MOTOR:** Intertwine the fingers of both open hands and pivot at the wrists a few times.

**NEED, HAVE TO, IMPERATIVE, MUST, NECESSARY, OUGHT TO, SHOULD, VITAL:** Move the right bent index finger firmly downward a few times.

**OUR:** Place the right slightly cupped hand on the right side of the chest with palm facing left. Move the right hand forward in a

circular motion, bringing it to rest near the left shoulder with the palm facing right.

**SALE, SELL, STORE:** Point both *and* hands down with bent wrists and pivot them in and out from the body a few times.

**STRIKE, REBELLION, REVOLT:** Hold up the right *S* hand at the right temple with palm facing out. Twist it sharply so that the palm faces out.

**TONIGHT:** Drop both bent hands down. Place the right wrist on the back of the left hand, and drop the right curved hand over the left hand. This sign combines the signs for *now* and *night.*

LOOK IN INDEX FOR LOCATION OF ADDITIONAL DESCRIPTIONS.

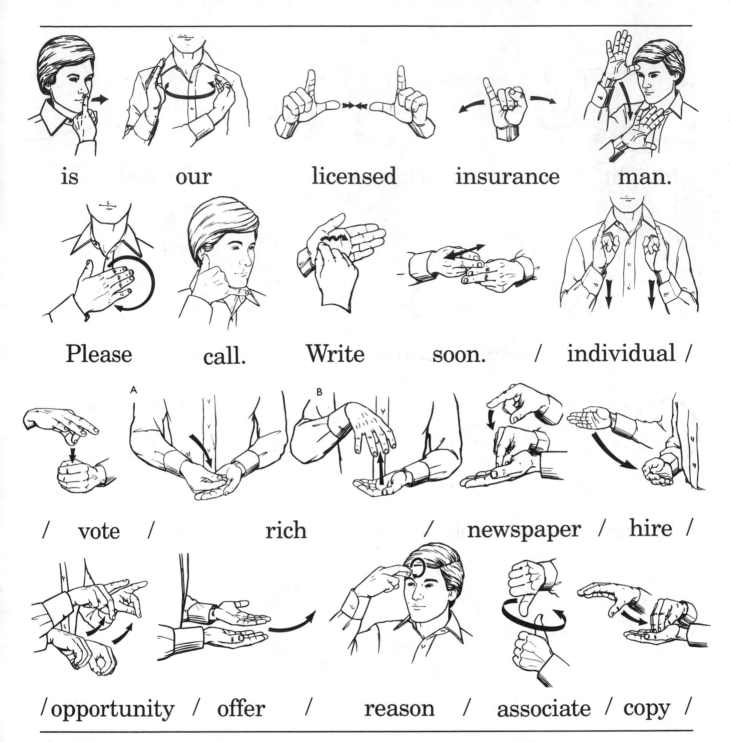

is          our          licensed     insurance          man.

Please          call.          Write          soon.     /     individual  /

/  vote  /          rich          /  newspaper  /  hire  /

/opportunity  /  offer  /          reason          /  associate  /  copy  /

**ASSOCIATE, EACH OTHER, FELLOW-SHIP, MINGLE, MUTUAL, ONE AN-OTHER, SOCIALIZE:** Point the left *A* thumb upward while the right *A* thumb points downward and revolves in a counterclockwise direction around the stationary left thumb.
**COPY, DUPLICATE, IMITATE:** Move the right open hand into the left flat palm while simultaneously closing into the *and* hand shape.
**HIRE, EMPLOY:** Swing the right flat (or *H*) hand in toward the waist with palm upward.
**INDIVIDUAL:** Drop both *I* hands simultaneously in front of the chest with palms facing.

**INSURANCE:** Shake the right *I* hand back and forth sideways.
**LICENSE:** Touch the *L* hand thumb tips a few times.
**MAN:** Touch the thumb of the right open hand on the forehead, then on the chest.
**NEWSPAPER:** This is the same sign as *printing*.
**OFFER, PRESENT, SUGGEST:** Move both palm-up flat hands forward and upward.
**OPPORTUNITY:** Hold both *O* hands to the front with palms down. Move both hands forward and up while forming *P* hands.
**REASON:** Make a counterclockwise circle

with the right *R* hand just in front of the forehead.
**RICH, WEALTHY:** Place the back of the right *and* hand in the left upturned palm; then lift it up a short distance into a palm-down curved open hand.
**SOON, SHORT (LENGTH OF TIME), BRIEF:** Cross the fingers of both *H* hands and rub the right *H* hand back and forth over the left index from fingertip to knuckle.
**VOTE, ELECT, ELECTION:** Place the thumb and index finger of the right *F* hand into the left *O* hand.
**WRITE:** Imitate writing on the left palm.

LOOK IN INDEX FOR LOCATION OF ADDITIONAL DESCRIPTIONS.

# Practice Giving Signs

Practice signing the following sentences once again. Try to do so without referring back to the illustrations. You can also cover the page opposite if you wish.

Improve business profits with ideas and advertising.

The secretary scheduled the assistant's appointment by telephone.

Doctors and lawyers usually receive good salaries.

Tom's work is building government housing.

Who is your new boss?

That letter has important advice about controlling the printing problem.

Your president gave an interesting speech.

I don't want to work late tonight.

The electricians decided to announce /cancel/ the strike.

Our library needs volunteers.

A new machine increased the farmer's sales.

Bob is our licensed insurance man.

Please call. Write soon.

/individual/vote/rich/newspaper/hire/ opportunity/offer/reason/associate/copy/

# Fingerspelling Practice

Practice the following words at least twice with a speed that is both steady and comfortable for you.

| | | | | | |
|---|---|---|---|---|---|
| kite | clap | keep | plot | drum | bean |
| wing | slap | weak | rank | slip | trip |
| leap | they | sink | each | plum | ship |
| fare | clip | glum | sent | thin | slim |
| deep | sing | tray | gone | what | brow |
| when | sock | skit | dash | salt | chat |
| than | went | comb | lane | fine | crib |

# Practice Receiving Signs

Interpret the following signs. Practicing by this method will help you receive and understand signs more easily. Say the words out loud as you proceed.

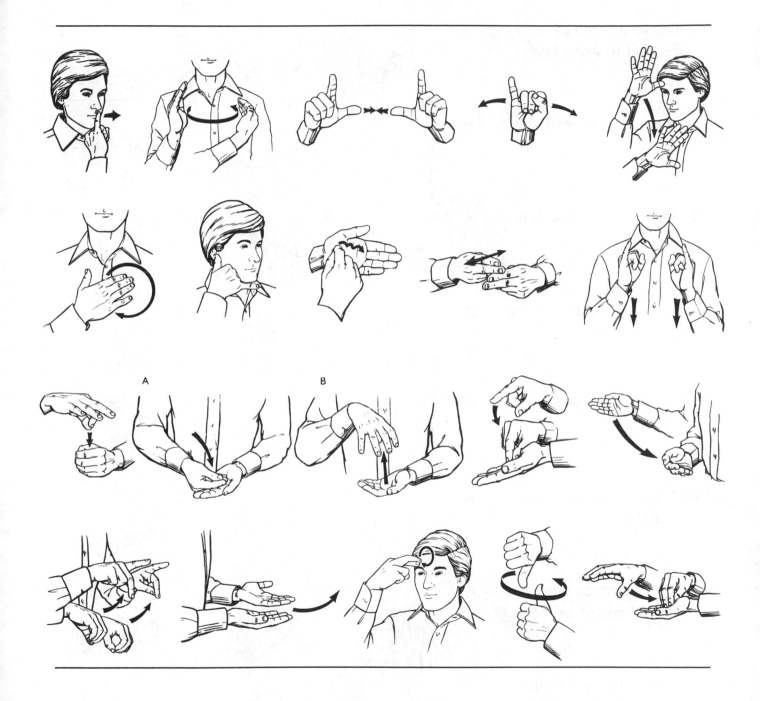

# Multiple Choice

Draw a circle around or place a check mark beside the sign that
matches the italicized word. For additional practice you can sign all
the words in the sentences.

1 The *new* electrician
decided to work late.

   A            B            C

2 The *president* will write
soon.

   A             B            C

3 He gave *advice* on the
telephone.

   A             B            C

4 His lawyer canceled the
*appointment*.

   A             B            C

5 Do you do *volunteer*
work?

   A             B            C

6 How is your newspaper
*business*?

   A             B            C

7 Our insurance man
worked on the *problem*.

   A             B            C

8 A new machine would
increase *profits*.

   A             B            C

# Test Your Skill: Matching

This section uses standard matching techniques. See if you can match the signs with the words by writing the correct word next to the sign.

1 _____

2 _____

3 _____

4 _____

5 _____

6 _____

7 _____

8 _____

9 _____

10 _____

11 _____

12 _____

13 _____

14 _____

late

work

library

farm

about

boss

need

idea

interest

imagination

give

schedule

important

salary

**15** 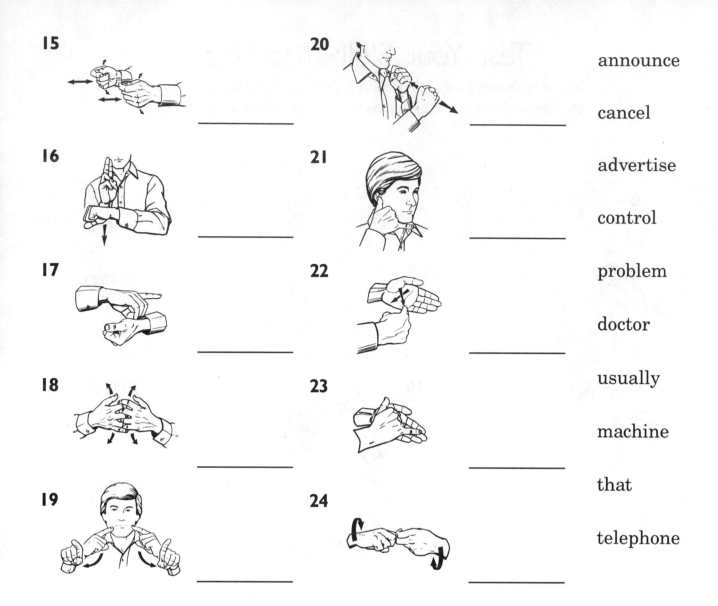 _____

**20** _____

announce

cancel

**16** _____

**21** _____

advertise

control

**17** _____

**22** _____

problem

doctor

**18** _____

**23** _____

usually

machine

**19** _____

**24** _____

that

telephone

# Extra Practice

Sign the following sentences which contain words chosen mainly from this chapter. This will give you additional practice using the signs you have just learned.

1 Please cancel my appointment with your boss.

2 Use your imagination to increase your opportunities.

3 What ideas do you have to improve business?

4 His lawyer smiled and gave him important advice.

5 I don't want to meet that negative individual.

6 Ask the secretary for our new schedule.

7 We need a licensed electrician to work on the house.

8 Eddy refused to work late.

9 We need some volunteer farm workers.

10 I decided to choose another doctor.

# Food

## 3

# Practice Learning Signs

Learn and practice the signs and sentences on each page before proceeding to the next. Descriptions are supplied at the bottom of each page.

I'm      hungry      for      bacon,

eggs,      toast,      and      coffee   / tea /

/ milk /      for      breakfast.      Please

**AM, ARE, BE, IS:** Place the right *A*-hand thumb on the lips and move the right hand straight forward. The other verbs are made with the same movement forward from the lips but are individually initialized. Use *R* for *are, B* for *be,* and *I* for *is.*

**BACON:** Touch the fingertips of both *U* hands in front of the chest. Move both hands out sideways in opposite directions while waving the *U* fingers up and down.

**BREAKFAST:** Move the fingers of the right closed *and* hand to the mouth a few times. Place the left flat hand into the bend of the right elbow; then raise the right forearm upward. *Note:* This sign is a combination of *eat* and *morning.*

**COFFEE:** Make a counterclockwise circular movement with the right *S* hand over the left *S* hand.

**EGG:** Bring the middle finger of the right *H* hand down upon the index finger of the left *H* and move both hands down and out. Most of the latter movement can be done from the wrists.

**FOR:** Touch the right temple with the right index finger; then dip it straight forward until the index finger is pointing forward.

**HUNGER, APPETITE, CRAVE, FAMINE, STARVE:** Move the thumb and fingers of the right *C* hand down the center of the chest from just below the throat.

**I:** Position the right *I* hand with palm facing left and thumb touching the chest.

**MILK:** Squeeze one or both slightly open *S* hands with a downward motion. Do it alternately if two hands are used.

**TEA:** Rotate the right thumb and index finger over the *O*-shape of the left hand.

**TOAST:** Thrust the right *V* fingers into the left palm, then into the back of the left flat hand.

LOOK IN INDEX FOR LOCATION OF ADDITIONAL DESCRIPTIONS.

put    knives,    forks,    spoons,    plates,

glasses,    cups,    napkins,    salt,    and

pepper    on    the    table.    For    supper

we    had    potatoes,    meat    /    fish    /,

**CUP:** Put the little-finger edge of the right *C* hand on the left flat palm.

**FISH (NOUN):** Place the fingertips of the left flat hand at the right wrist, and then swing the right hand back and forth from the wrist.

**FORK:** Move the fingers of the right *V* hand into the left upturned palm a few times. *Note:* Sometimes the three fingers of the right *M* hand are used.

**GLASS (DRINKING):** Place the little-finger edge of the right *C* hand on the left flat palm and raise the right hand a short distance.

**KNIFE:** Move the right *H* (or index) fingers downward across the left *H* (or index) fingers several times.

**MEAT, BEEF:** Using the right thumb and index finger, pinch the flesh of the left flat hand between the thumb and index finger.

**ON:** Bring the right flat hand down onto the back of the left flat hand.

**POTATO:** Strike the tips of the right curved *V* fingers on the back of the left downturned *S* hand.

**PUT:** Imitate picking something up at the left and moving it to the right.

**SALT:** Tap the right *V* fingers on the left *H* fingers a few times.

**SPOON:** Lift the right curved *H* fingers up toward the mouth a few times from the palm of the left slightly curved hand.

**SUPPER:** First sign *eat:* Move the closed

right *and* hand toward the mouth a few times. Then sign *night:* Place the right wrist on the back of left palm-down flat hand, and drop the right curved hand over the left.

**TABLE:** Fold the arms with the right hand on top of the left forearm. Pat the left forearm.

**WE, US:** Touch the right index finger on the right shoulder; then move it in a forward semicircle until it touches the left shoulder. Often the *W* or *U* hand is used instead of the index finger to indicate either *we* or *us,* respectively.

LOOK IN INDEX FOR LOCATION OF ADDITIONAL DESCRIPTIONS.

gravy,    bread,    butter,    and    water.

Dessert    was    cake    or    apple

pie    with    vanilla / chocolate / ice cream.

Today's    lunch    is

**APPLE:** Pivot the knuckle of the right closed index finger back and forth on the right cheek.

**BREAD:** Draw the little-finger edge of the right hand downward a few times over the back of the flat left hand which has its palm facing the body.

**BUTTER:** Quickly brush the fingertips of the right *H* hand across the left palm a few times.

**CAKE:** Move the fingertips and thumb of the right *C* hand forward across the left flat hand from wrist to fingertips.

**CHOCOLATE:** Make a few small counterclockwise circles with the thumb of the

right *C* hand over the back of the left flat hand.

**DESSERT:** Bring the thumbs of both upright *D* hands together a few times.

**GRAVY, FAT, GREASE, OIL:** Pull the right index and thumb down from holding the left hand a few times.

**ICE CREAM, LOLLIPOP:** Pull the right *S* hand to the mouth with a downward twist a few times. The tongue may be shown.

**LUNCH:** First sign *eat*; then sign *noon*: Place the left flat hand at the outer bend of the right elbow and raise the right forearm to an upright position with palm facing left.

**OR, EITHER:** Point the index of the left *L*

hand forward with palm facing right. Move the right index from the tip of the left thumb to the top of the left index a few times.

**PIE:** Pull the right little-finger edge across the left palm twice at different angles.

**TODAY:** Drop both *Y* (or flat) hands together in front of the chest. Point the left index to the right with palm down. Rest the right elbow on the left index and point the right index upward. Move the right arm in a partial arc across the body from right to left. This sign can also be done by combining either *now* and *day,* or *this* and *day.*

**WATER:** Touch the mouth with the index finger of the right *W* hand a few times.

LOOK IN INDEX FOR LOCATION OF ADDITIONAL DESCRIPTIONS.

soup,　　cheese,　　and　　crackers.　　Fruits

I　　like　　best　　are　　bananas,

strawberries,　grapes,　peaches,　　pears,　　and

oranges.　　Let's　　　　get　　a　hamburger,

**BANANA:** Peel an imaginary banana using the left index finger as the model.

**BEST:** Touch the lips with the fingers of the right flat hand; then, while closing it into an *A*-hand shape, move it to the right side of the head above head level.

**CHEESE:** Place the heels of both hands together and rotate them back and forth in opposite directions.

**CRACKER:** Strike the right *S* hand near the left elbow.

**FRUIT:** Place the thumb and index fingers of the right *F* hand on the right cheek. Twist forward or backward.

**GRAPES:** Place the fingertips of the right curved hand on the back of the left closed hand. Move the right hand down on the left hand with several small hops.

**HAMBURGER:** Cup the right hand on top of the left cupped hand; then reverse.

**LET, ALLOW, GRANT, PERMIT:** Hold both flat hands forward with palms facing. Swing them up simultaneously so that the fingertips point slightly out. The *L* hands may be used for *let* and the *P* hands for *permit*.

**LIKE, ADMIRE:** Place the right thumb and index finger against the chest, with the other fingers extended. Bring the thumb and index finger together as the hand is moved a short distance forward.

**ORANGE (COLOR AND FRUIT):** Slightly open and squeeze the right *S* hand in front of the mouth a few times.

**PEACH:** Touch the right cheek with the fingertips of the right open hand; then draw it down a short distance while simultaneously forming the *and* hand.

**PEAR:** Slide the right hand over the left to the right; end with both *and* hand shapes.

**SOUP:** Hold the left curved hand with palm facing up; then move the slightly curved right *H* fingers into the left palm and upward a few times.

**STRAWBERRY:** Grasp the left index finger with the right thumb and fingers and twist back and forth.

LOOK IN INDEX FOR LOCATION OF ADDITIONAL DESCRIPTIONS.

French fries,     and          soda.     Which     restaurant

has       the       most     delicious     pizza / food / ?

Carol's             spaghetti,     lemon          cream

pies,               and          cookies     are     delicious.

---

**COOKIE, BISCUIT:** Place the right *C* thumb and fingertips into the left flat palm and twist. Repeat a few times. *Note:* The sign for *biscuit* makes the right hand rise a few times but not twist.

**CREAM:** Move the little-finger edge of the right curved hand across the left flat palm from fingertips to wrist.

**DELICIOUS:** Touch the lips with the right middle finger. Sometimes, in addition to the first part of the sign, the middle finger and thumb are rubbed together a few times as the hand moves forward.

**FOOD, CONSUME, DINE, EAT, MEAL:** The right *and* hand moves toward the mouth a few times.

**FRENCH FRIES:** Sign the right *F* hand once, then again a second time slightly to the right.

**LEMON:** Hold the thumb of the right *L* hand at the lips. Assume an expression indicating sourness.

**MOST:** Touch the fingertips of both *and* hands together before the chest with palms facing down (the sign for *more*). Move the right hand up while forming the *A* hand. *Alternative:* Place both *A* hands together in front of the chest with palms facing, and raise the right hand.

**PIZZA:** Outline the shape of a *Z* in front of the chest with the *P* hand.

**RESTAURANT:** With the palm facing left,

move the right *R* fingers from the right to the left of the mouth.

**SODA, POP, SODA WATER:** Put the thumb and index finger of the right *F* hand into the left *O* hand. Open the right hand and slap the left *O* with it.

**SPAGHETTI, STRING, THREAD, WIRE:** Touch the tips of both *I* fingers; then make small spirals as both hands are drawn apart to the sides.

**WHICH, EITHER, WHETHER:** With the palms facing, move the *A* hands alternately up and down in front of the chest.

LOOK IN INDEX FOR LOCATION OF ADDITIONAL DESCRIPTIONS.

We ate chicken sandwiches and

doughnuts. Ed doesn't drink beer

/ liquor /. / taste / thirsty / fasting / candy /

/ refrigerator / cook (verb) / smell / popcorn / bake /

**BAKE, OVEN:** Slide the right flat (or *B*) hand under the left downturned flat hand.
**BEER:** Draw the index-finger side of the right *B* hand down at the right side of the mouth.
**CANDY, SUGAR:** Brush the tips of the right *U* fingers downward over the lips and chin a few times.
**CHICKEN, HEN:** Open and close the right index finger and thumb in front of the mouth. Sometimes these fingers are also brought down into the upturned left palm with a pecking motion.
**COOK (VERB), COOK (NOUN), FRY:** Place first the palm side and then the back of the right flat hand on the upturned palm of

the left flat hand. To sign *cook* as a noun, add the sign for *person* (personalizing word ending).
**DOUGHNUT:** Beginning at the lips, make a forward circle with both *R* hands.
**DRINK:** Move the right *C* hand in a short arc toward the mouth.
**FASTING:** Move the right thumb and index side of the *F* hand across the mouth from left to right.
**LIQUOR, WHISKEY:** Strike the back of the left closed hand with the extended little finger of the right hand a few times while keeping the right index finger extended.
**POPCORN:** Hold both *S* hands in front with

the palms facing up. Flick both index fingers up alternately several times.
**REFRIGERATOR:** Shake both *R* hands.
**SANDWICH:** Place the fingertips of both palm-to-palm hands near the mouth.
**TASTE:** Touch the tip of the tongue with the right middle finger. The other fingers of the right open hand are extended.
**THIRSTY, PARCHED:** With the palm facing in, trace a downward line with the right index finger by starting under the chin and ending near the base of the neck.

LOOK IN INDEX FOR LOCATION OF ADDITIONAL DESCRIPTIONS.

# Practice Giving Signs

Practice signing the following sentences once again. Try to do so without referring back to the illustrations. You can also cover the page opposite if you wish.

I'm hungry for bacon, eggs, toast, and coffee /tea/milk/ for breakfast.

Please put knives, forks, spoons, plates, glasses, cups, napkins, salt, and pepper on the table.

For supper we had potatoes, meat /fish/, gravy, bread, butter, and water.

Dessert was cake or apple pie with vanilla /chocolate/ ice cream.

Today's lunch is soup, cheese, and crackers.

Fruits I like best are bananas, strawberries, grapes, peaches, pears, and oranges.

Let's get a hamburger, French fries, and soda.

Which restaurant has the most delicious pizza /food/?

Carol's spaghetti, lemon cream pies, and cookies are delicious.

We ate chicken sandwiches and doughnuts.

Ed doesn't drink beer/liquor/.

/taste/thirsty/fasting/candy/refrigerator/ cook (verb)/smell/popcorn/bake/

# Fingerspelling Practice

Practice the following words at least twice with a speed that is both steady and comfortable for you.

| | | | | | |
|---|---|---|---|---|---|
| milk | slow | spit | blink | thing | twist |
| moat | drop | blot | crash | phone | skate |
| clap | crab | flip | clock | drown | brick |
| brew | chip | swim | shape | brave | style |
| then | sack | plan | slide | think | smart |
| ship | glue | grin | where | trial | swans |
| clan | free | trim | cheap | plane | grape |

# Practice Receiving Signs

Interpret the following signs. Practicing by this method will help you receive and understand the signs more easily. Say the words out loud as you proceed.

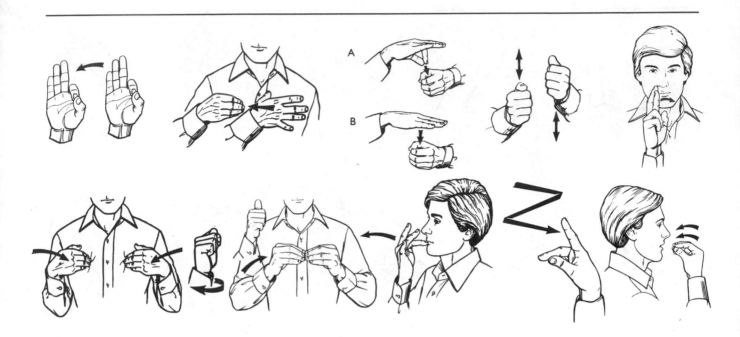

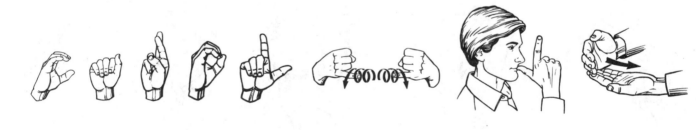

# Extra Practice

Sign the following sentences which contain words chosen mainly from this chapter. This will give you additional practice using the signs you have just learned.

1 The strawberry ice cream soda tasted delicious.

2 Something smells good in the kitchen.

3 We ate potatoes, chicken, and gravy at Mom's house.

4 Do you have knives, forks, and spoons on the table?

5 We decided not to eat hamburgers and French fries for lunch.

6 I like salt but not pepper with my food.

7 My favorite food for breakfast is bananas, pears, or oranges.

8 You can have cake or apple pie for dessert.

9 Please come to our house for spaghetti dinner.

10 I'm hungry and thirsty.

# Test Your Skill: Matching

This section uses standard matching techniques. See if you can match the signs with the words by writing the correct word next to the sign.

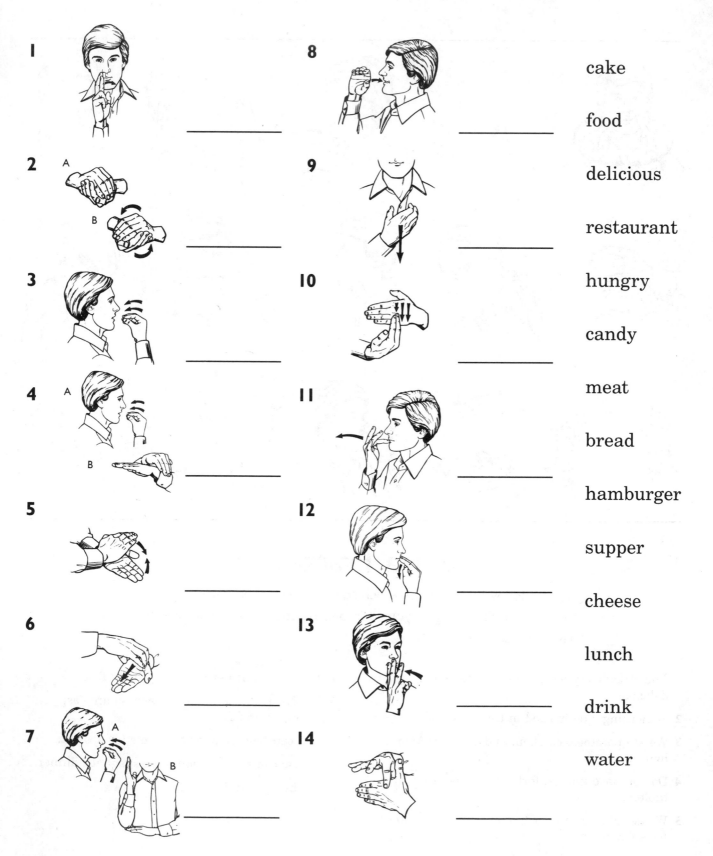

1 _____

2 _____

3 _____

4 _____

5 _____

6 _____

7 _____

8 _____

9 _____

10 _____

11 _____

12 _____

13 _____

14 _____

cake

food

delicious

restaurant

hungry

candy

meat

bread

hamburger

supper

cheese

lunch

drink

water

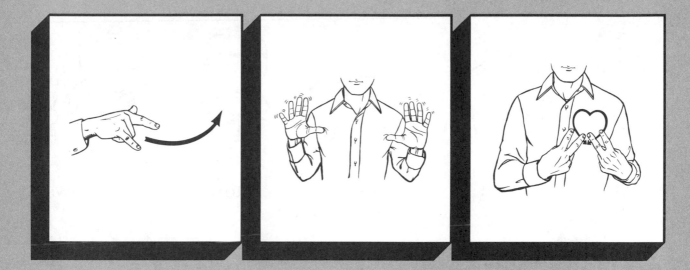

# Travel
# and
# Holidays

# Practice Learning Signs

Learn and practice the signs and sentences on each page before proceeding to the next. Descriptions are supplied at the bottom of each page.

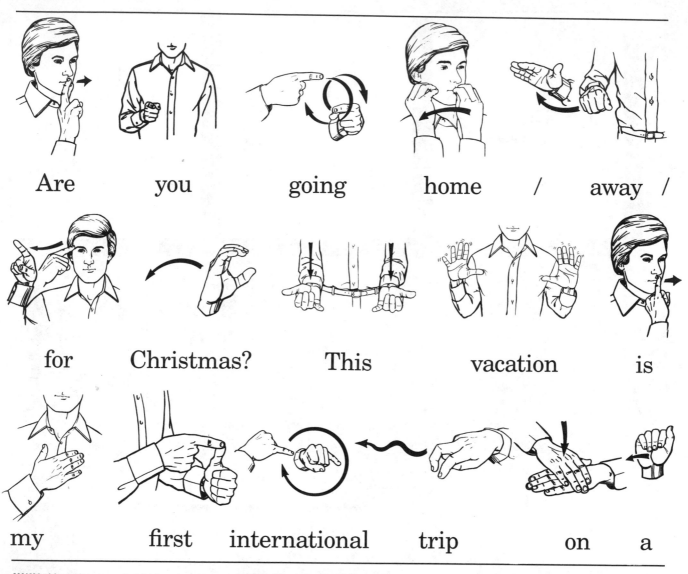

Are you going home / away /

for Christmas? This vacation is

my first international trip on a

**AWAY:** Move the curved right hand away from the body and to the right, ending with the palm facing forward and downward. Sometimes the *A* hand is used at the beginning of the sign.

**CHRISTMAS:** Move the right *C* hand in a sideways arc to the right with the palm facing forward.

**FIRST:** Touch the extended left *A* thumb with the right index finger.

**FOR:** Touch the right temple with the right index finger; then dip it straight forward until the index finger is pointing forward.

**GO:** Point both index fingers toward each other and rotate them around each other as they are moved away from the body.

**HOME:** Place the fingertips of the right *and* hand first at the mouth, then at the right cheek. Sometimes the position at the cheek is made with a slightly curved hand.

**INTERNATIONAL:** Point the little finger of the left *I* hand forward with the palm facing down. With the palm facing down, rotate the right *I* hand forward around the left *I* hand.

**THIS:** Put the right index fingertip into the palm of the left flat hand if something specific is indicated. Drop both *Y* (or flat) hands together with palms facing up if something more abstract is indicated. Sometimes the right *Y* hand by itself is moved downward with palm facing down.

**TRIP, JOURNEY, TRAVEL:** With right palm

facing down, imitate traveling along a winding road with right curved *V* fingers.

**VACATION, HOLIDAY, LEISURE:** Place both thumbs at the armpits and wiggle all the fingers.

LOOK IN INDEX FOR LOCATION OF ADDITIONAL DESCRIPTIONS.

plane / ship /. Our friends will

fly out of the country for

two weeks. Check the car for

gas / oil / before leaving for

**BEFORE (TIME):** Hold the slightly curved left hand out to the front with palm facing in. Hold the right curved hand near the palm of the left and then draw the right hand in toward the body.

**CAR, AUTOMOBILE, DRIVE:** Use both closed hands to manipulate an imaginary steering wheel.

**CHECK, EXAMINE, INVESTIGATE, RESEARCH:** Point the right index finger to the right eye, then move it forward and down, and then forward across the upturned left palm until it goes beyond the fingers. The *R* hand is often used for *research*.

**COUNTRY (NATIONAL TERRITORY):** Rub the palm side of the right *Y* hand in a counterclockwise direction on the underside of the left forearm near the elbow.

**FRIEND, FRIENDSHIP:** Interlock the right and left index fingers and repeat in reverse.

**GASOLINE:** Bring the right *A* thumb down into the left *O* hand.

**LEAVE, DEPART, RETIRE, WITHDRAW:** Bring both flat hands up from the right and close to *A* hands.

**OUT:** Draw the right closed hand up, through, and out of the left *C* hand.

**PLANE, FLY:** Use the *Y* hand with index finger extended and palm facing down. Make a forward-upward sweeping motion.

**SHIP:** Put the right *3* hand on the palm of the left curved hand and move both hands

forward simultaneously with a wavy motion.

**TWO:** Hold up the right index and middle fingers to indicate the number 2. *Note:* See "Numbers" on page 15 for complete listing.

**WEEK, LAST WEEK, NEXT WEEK:** Move the right index-finger hand across the left flat palm in a forward movement. For *last week,* let the right hand continue in an upward-backward direction to the right shoulder. *Week* and *past* can also be used to sign *last week.* For *next week,* let the right hand continue beyond the left hand and point forward.

**WILL (VERB), SHALL:** Place right flat hand opposite right temple or cheek with palm facing in. Move hand straight ahead.

LOOK IN INDEX FOR LOCATION OF ADDITIONAL DESCRIPTIONS.

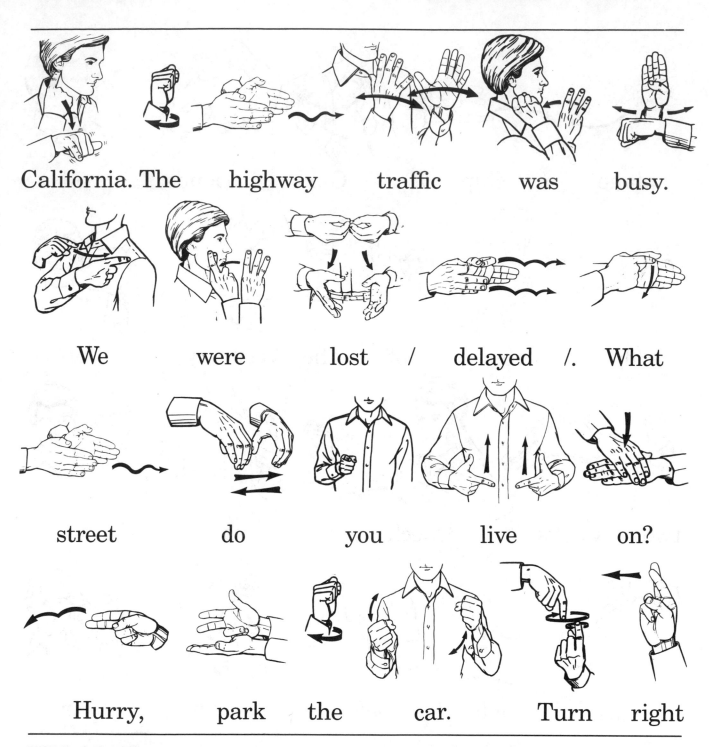

California. The highway traffic was busy.

We were lost / delayed /. What

street do you live on?

Hurry, park the car. Turn right

**BUSY:** Tap the wrist of the left closed palm-down hand with the wrist of the right *B* hand which has palm facing forward. The right hand moves from right to left as it taps the left wrist.

**CALIFORNIA, GOLD:** Touch the right ear, then shake the right palm-down *Y* hand.

**DELAY, POSTPONE, PROCRASTINATE, PUT OFF:** Place both *F* hands to the front with palms facing and fingers pointing forward. Make a few short forward arcs.

**DO, ACTION, CONDUCT, DEED, DONE, PERFORM:** Point both *C* hands down to the front and move them simultaneously first to one side and then the other.

**HIGHWAY, AVENUE, PATH, ROAD, STREET, WAY:** Hold both flat hands with palms facing; then move them forward together while simultaneously winding from side to side. *Note:* All these words may be signed by using the initial. Thus, *avenue* could be signed with *A* hands, and so on.

**HURRY, HUSTLE, RUSH:** Move one or both *H* hands quickly forward in short arcs. *Note:* If two hands are used, they can be quickly raised up and down alternately.

**LIVE, ADDRESS, DWELL, RESIDE:** Move the palm sides of both *L* (or *A*) hands up from the abdomen to the chest.

**LOST, LOSE:** Hold the fingertips of both

palm-up *and* hands together; then separate the hands by dropping them down and opening them.

**PARK:** Bring the right *3* hand down onto the left flat palm. Movements suggesting the parking of a vehicle can also be made with the right *3* hand on the left palm.

**TRAFFIC:** With the palms facing, move the open hands back and forth a few times.

**TURN:** Revolve the right index finger around the left index finger in counterclockwise circles while simultaneously turning the left index slowly in the same direction.

LOOK IN INDEX FOR LOCATION OF ADDITIONAL DESCRIPTIONS.

at　　the　　next　　corner,　　then　　first

left　　toward　　the　　ocean.　　Canoeing

is　　fun.　　/　empty　/　full　/

/ ride (in a vehicle) / across / send / pass / valentine /

**ACROSS, CROSS, OVER:** With the left flat hand facing down, move the little-finger edge of the right flat hand over the knuckles of the left hand.

**AT:** Bring the fingers of the right flat hand in contact with the back of the left flat hand. This sign is often fingerspelled.

**CANOEING:** Hold right *S* hand over left *S* hand to right or left of body. Move hands simultaneously down and backward.

**CORNER:** Point the flat-hand fingers or the index fingers at right angles to each other.

**EMPTY, BARE, NAKED, VACANT:** Place the right middle finger on the back of the left downturned hand and move it from the wrist to beyond the knuckles.

**FULL, FILLED:** Slide the right flat hand left over the top of the left closed hand.

**FUN:** Brush tip of nose with fingers of right *U* hand. Move the right *U* hand down and brush the left and right *U* fingers up and down against each other a few times.

**NEXT:** Hold both flat hands to the front with palms facing in and right hand behind left. Move right hand over to front of left.

**OCEAN, SEA:** Touch the mouth with the index finger of the right *W* hand a few times (the sign for *water*). Move both downturned curved hands forward with a wavy motion.

**PASS:** Pass the right *A* hand forward from behind the left *A* hand.

**RIDE (IN A VEHICLE):** Place the right

curved *U* fingers in the left *O* hand and move both hands forward.

**SEND:** Touch the back of the left bent hand with the fingertips of the right bent hand; then swing the right hand forward.

**THEN:** Point the left *L* hand forward with palm facing right; then touch the left thumb and index finger with the right index finger.

**TOWARD, TO:** Hold the left index finger up and move the right index finger toward it until the fingertips touch.

**VALENTINE:** Outline a heart shape on the chest with the fingers of both *V* hands.

LOOK IN INDEX FOR LOCATION OF ADDITIONAL DESCRIPTIONS.

# Practice Giving Signs

Practice signing the following sentences once again. Try to do so without referring back to the illustrations. You can also cover the page opposite if you wish.

Are you going home /away/ for Christmas?

This vacation is my first international trip on a plane /ship/.

Our friends will fly out of the country for two weeks.

Check the car for gas /oil/ before leaving for California.

The highway traffic was busy.

We were lost /delayed/.

What street do you live on?

Hurry, park the car.

Turn right at the next corner, then first left toward the ocean.

Canoeing is fun.

/empty/full/ride (in a vehicle)/across/send/pass/ valentine/

# Fingerspelling Practice

Practice the following words at least twice with a speed that is both steady and comfortable for you.

| | | | | | |
|---|---|---|---|---|---|
| John | George | Mark | Donna | Michael | Karen |
| Patty | Sherry | Roderic | Timothy | Julie | Geoffrey |
| Doug | Sam | Joanna | David | Roger | Glenda |
| Maria | Christine | Robbie | Tony | Gayla | Mickey |
| Wendell | Vickie | Austin | Lisa | Kenny | Harold |
| Susan | Lonnie | Charlie | Terri | Sandy | Nancy |
| Phil | Paul | Theresa | Jeff | Jack | Stephen |

# Practice Receiving Signs

Interpret the following signs. Practicing by this method will help you receive and understand the signs more easily. Say the words out loud as you proceed.

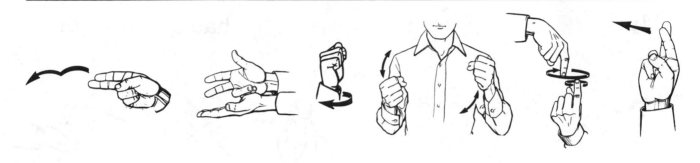

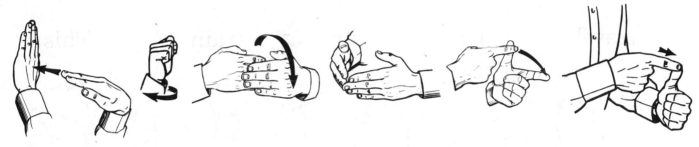

A          B

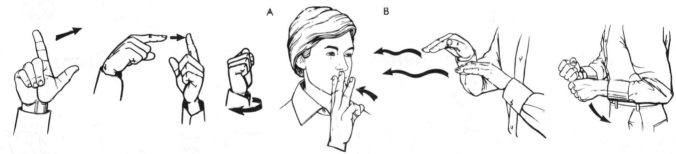

A          B

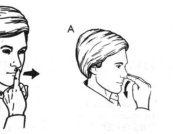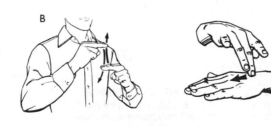

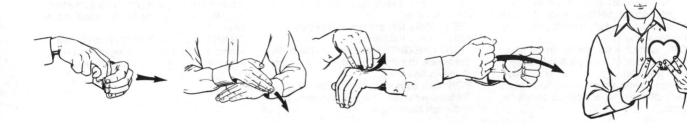

# Practice Learning Signs (continued)

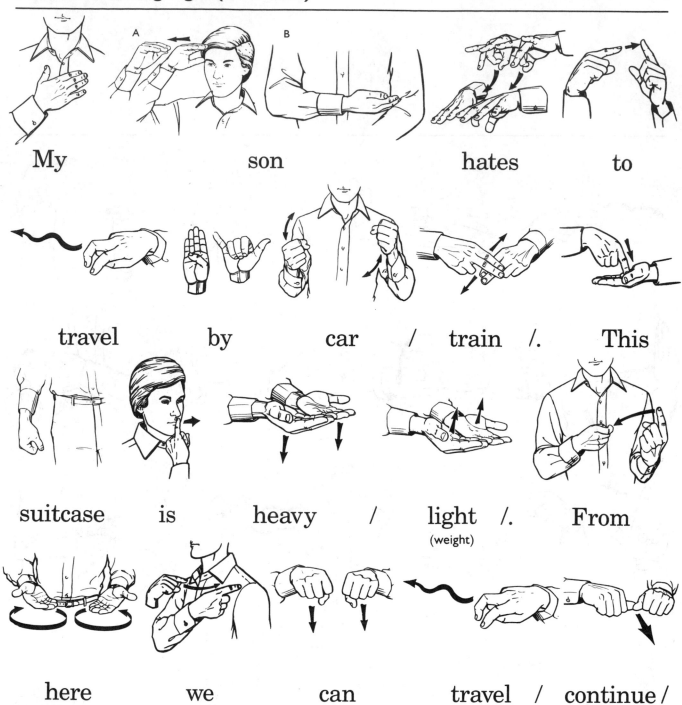

My          son          hates          to

travel          by          car          /          train          /.          This

suitcase          is          heavy          /          light          /.          From

here          we          can          travel          /          continue /

**CAN, ABILITY, ABLE, CAPABLE, COMPETENT, COULD, POSSIBLE:** Hold both S (or A) hands to the front and move them down firmly together.
**CONTINUE, ENDURE, LASTING, PERMANENT, PERSEVERE:** Place the tip of the right A thumb behind the left A thumb and move both hands forward together. The palms face down.
**FROM:** Touch the upright left index finger with the knuckle of the right X index finger; then move the right hand in a slight backward-downward arc. *Note:* Sometimes the left index finger is crooked or pointed forward.

**HATE, ABHOR, DESPISE, DETEST, LOATHE:** Hold both open hands in front of the chest with palms facing down, and flick both middle fingers outward simultaneously.
**HEAVY, WEIGHTY:** Hold both flat hands to the front with palms up and drop them a short distance.
**HERE:** Make forward-outward circles with both palm-up flat hands.
**LIGHT (WEIGHT):** Hold both flat hands to the front with palms up and raise them up slightly a few times.
**SON:** First sign *male;* then move the right flat hand with palm facing up into the crook of the left bent elbow.

**SUITCASE:** Use the right hand to imitate the movement of picking up a suitcase.
**THIS (SPECIFIC):** Put the right index finger into the left palm.
**TRAIN, RAILROAD:** With palms facing down, rub the right H fingers back and forth over the length of the left H fingers a few times.
**TRAVEL, JOURNEY, TRIP:** With right palm facing down, imitate traveling along a winding road with right curved V fingers.

LOOK IN INDEX FOR LOCATION OF ADDITIONAL DESCRIPTIONS.

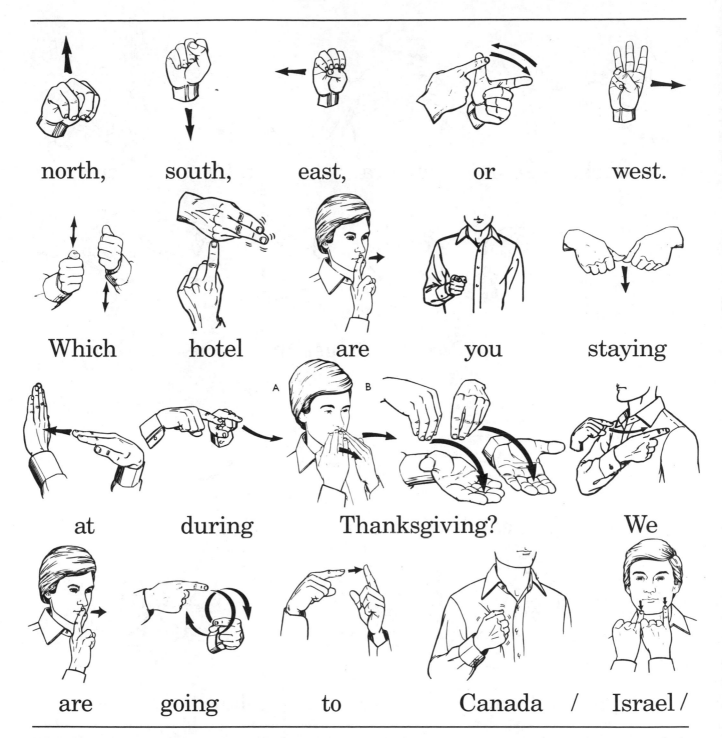

north,     south,     east,          or          west.

Which     hotel     are     you     staying

at     during     Thanksgiving?     We

are     going     to     Canada / Israel /

**CANADA, CANADIAN:** Grasp the right jacket or coat lapel (or an imaginary one) and shake it.
**DURING, IN THE MEANTIME, WHILE:** Point both index-finger hands forward with palms down and a small distance between them. Move them forward simultaneously in a slight down-forward-up curve.
**EAST:** Move the right *E* hand to the right with palm facing forward.
**HOTEL:** Rest the little-finger edge of the right *H* hand on the left index finger while moving the *H* fingers back and forth.
**ISRAEL:** Using the palm side of the right *I*

finger, stroke downward at each side of the chin.
**NORTH:** Move the *N* hand upward.
**OR, EITHER:** Point the index finger of the left *L* hand forward with palm facing right. Move the right index finger from the tip of the left thumb to the top of the left index finger a few times.
**SOUTH:** Move the *S* hand downward with palm facing forward.
**STAY, REMAIN:** Place the tip of the right *A* thumb on top of the left *A* thumb and move both hands downward together. *Alternative:*

Move either one *Y* hand (or both) firmly downward.
**THANKSGIVING:** Sign *thanks. Giving,* or *give,* is signed by moving both palm-down *and* hands forward to a flat open-hand and palm-up position.
**WEST:** Move the *W* hand to the left.
**WHICH:** Move both *A* hands alternately up and down with palms facing.

LOOK IN INDEX FOR LOCATION OF ADDITIONAL DESCRIPTIONS.

next week. Your camera takes clear

pictures. Get out of / get in / the boat.

/ carry / earth / nation / place / near /

/ foreign / stamps / far / follow / gone /

**BOAT:** Move cupped hands forward with wavy motion.

**CARRY, TRANSPORT:** Hold both slightly curved hands to front with palms facing up. Move both hands in an arc from right to left, or vice versa.

**CLEAR, BRIGHT, LIGHT, LUMINOUS, OBVIOUS:** Hold both *and* hands at chest level with palms down. Open hands while moving them up and to the sides with palms facing forward.

**EARTH, GEOGRAPHY, GLOBE, TERRESTRIAL:** Grasp the back of the left closed hand between the right index finger and thumb. Pivot the right hand from left to right toward the left fingers and elbow.

**FAR, DISTANT, REMOTE:** Move the right *A* hand well forward from beside the left *A* hand.

**NATION, NATIONAL, NATURE, NATURAL:** Make a clockwise circle above the back of the left *S* hand with right extended *N* fingers, then bring the *N* fingers down on the back of the left hand.

**NEAR, ADJACENT, BY, CLOSE TO:** Hold the left curved hand away from the body with palm facing in. Move the back of the right curved hand from close to the body to near the palm of the left hand.

**PICTURE, PHOTOGRAPH:** Hold the right *C* hand close to the face, then move it forward until the thumb side of the right *C* hand

is against the left flat palm.

**PLACE, AREA, LOCATION, SITE:** With palms facing, hold both *P* hands a short distance in front of the chest and touch the middle fingers. Make a circle toward self with both hands and touch the middle fingertips again. For *area* use *A*, for *location* use *L*, for *site* use *S*.

**STAMPS (POSTAL):** With palm facing in, touch the lips with the right *U* fingers, then place the *U* fingers palm down on the left palm.

LOOK IN INDEX FOR LOCATION OF ADDITIONAL DESCRIPTIONS.

# Practice Giving Signs

Practice signing the following sentences once again. Try to do so without referring back to the illustrations. You can also cover the page opposite if you wish.

My son hates to travel by car /train/.

This suitcase is heavy /light/.

From here we can travel /continue/ north, south, east, or west.

Which hotel are you staying at during Thanksgiving?

We are going to Canada /Israel/ next week.

Your camera takes clear pictures.

Get out of /get in/ the boat.

/carry/earth/nation/place/near/foreign/stamps/ far/follow/gone/

# Vocabulary Review

Identify the following signs from this and previous chapters to reinforce your vocabulary.

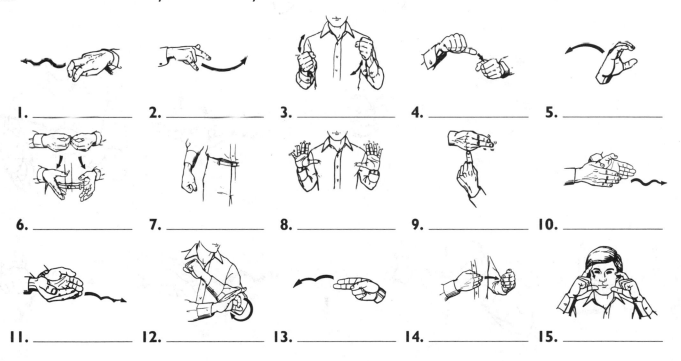

1. _____
2. _____
3. _____
4. _____
5. _____
6. _____
7. _____
8. _____
9. _____
10. _____
11. _____
12. _____
13. _____
14. _____
15. _____

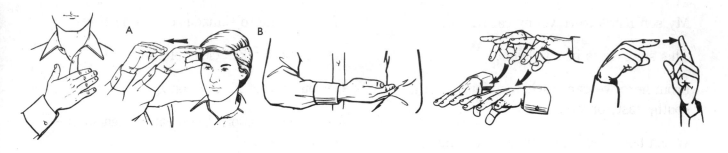

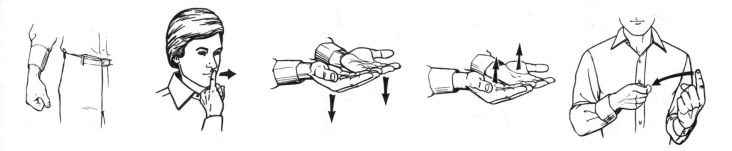

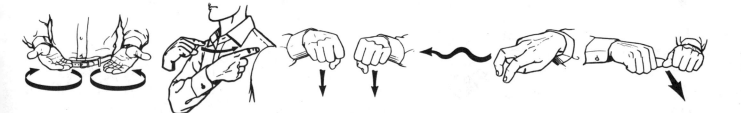

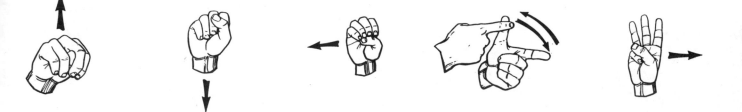

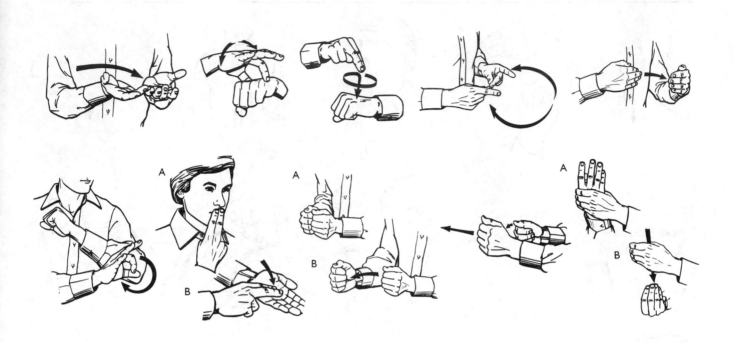

# Multiple Choice

Draw a circle around or place a check mark beside the sign that matches the italicized word. For additional practice you can sign all the words in the sentences.

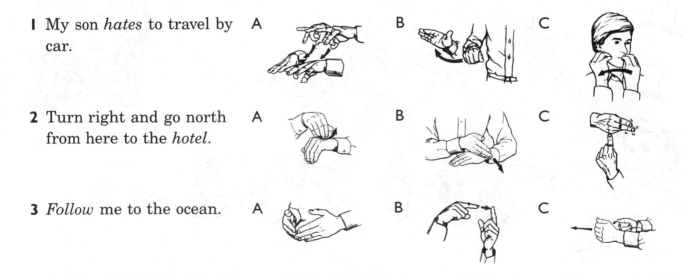

1 My son *hates* to travel by car.    A    B    C

2 Turn right and go north from here to the *hotel*.    A    B    C

3 *Follow* me to the ocean.    A    B    C

**4** Take your camera to Mom's *during* Thanksgiving holiday.

A  B  C

**5** Our friends are flying *home* for Christmas.

A  B  C

**6** Ray said the *traffic* on the highway was busy.

A  B  C

**7** Do you live on Main *Street*?

A  B  C

**8** Did you buy anything for your *valentine*?

A  B  C

**9** The train was late and we were *delayed*.

A  B  C

**10** My friend sent a letter about her *international* trip to Israel.

A  B  C

**11** Come for a *ride* in the car with me.

A  B  C

**12** We went *across* the ocean by ship.

A  B  C

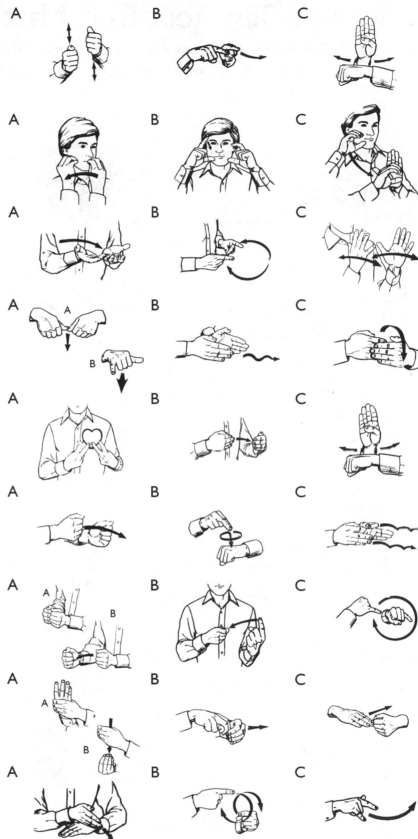

# Test Your Skill: Matching

This section uses standard matching techniques. See if you can match the signs with the words by writing the correct word next to the sign.

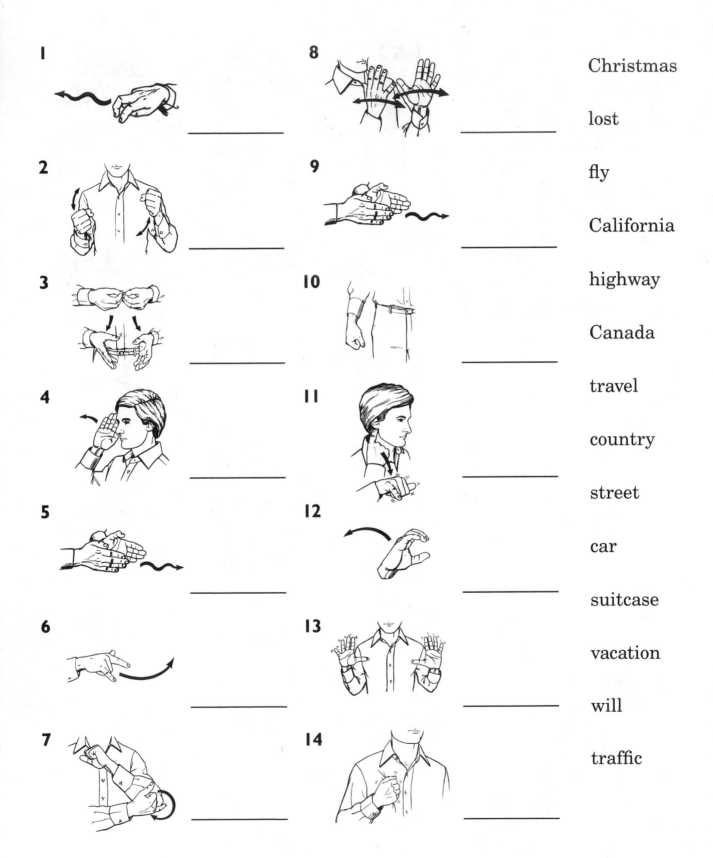

1 _____

2 _____

3 _____

4 _____

5 _____

6 _____

7 _____

8 _____

9 _____

10 _____

11 _____

12 _____

13 _____

14 _____

Christmas

lost

fly

California

highway

Canada

travel

country

street

car

suitcase

vacation

will

traffic

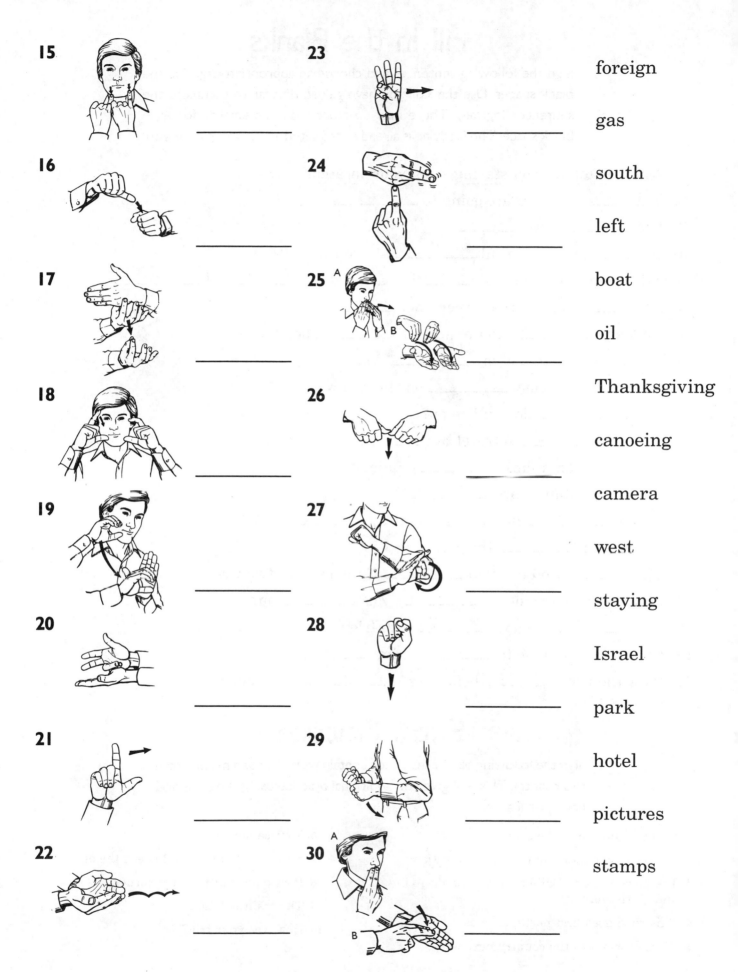

**15** _____

**16** _____

**17** _____

**18** _____

**19** _____

**20** _____

**21** _____

**22** _____

**23** _____

**24** _____

**25** _____

**26** _____

**27** _____

**28** _____

**29** _____

**30** _____

foreign

gas

south

left

boat

oil

Thanksgiving

canoeing

camera

west

staying

Israel

park

hotel

pictures

stamps

# Fill In the Blanks

Sign the following sentences and choose an appropriate sign for the blank spaces. Use the skill you have gained thus far to complete the sentences logically. There may be more than one answer for each blank space. The first one is already completed as an example for you.

1. Which <u>hotel</u> are you <u>staying</u> at on your <u>vacation</u>?
2. Is it _____ you are going to _____?
3. The _____ is _____.
4. _____ is a beautiful _____ to live in.
5. Before starting your _____ the car needs _____ and _____.
6. Turn _____ at the corner, then _____.
7. We travel _____ to Canada for _____ holiday.
8. I took a _____ of my _____ John.
9. I don't like the busy _____ on the highway.
10. What _____ do you live on?
11. My son _____ to travel by _____ or _____.
12. He is going on a (an) _____ trip for two _____.
13. _____ stamps are _____.
14. We got _____ in the busy highway _____.
15. Hurry and _____ the car.
16. We _____ on our trip _____ California for two weeks.
17. What is the name of the _____ you _____ on?
18. It is _____ to go _____ with friends.
19. My uncle wants me to _____ him _____.
20. Park the car _____ before we _____ into the house.

# Extra Practice

Sign the following sentences which contain words chosen mainly from this chapter. This will give you additional practice using the signs you have just learned.

1 Is your suitcase in the car?
2 I'm going home to Canada for my vacation.
3 They are going to California for Thanksgiving and Christmas.
4 This road goes first north, then east.
5 We will travel to the country next week.
6 Your camera is lost.
7 Stay in the car while I check the oil.
8 Please park at the next corner.
9 The train is late.
10 How was your trip?

# Sports
# and
# Recreation

5

# Practice Learning Signs

Learn and practice the signs and sentences on each page before proceeding to the next. Descriptions are supplied at the bottom of each page.

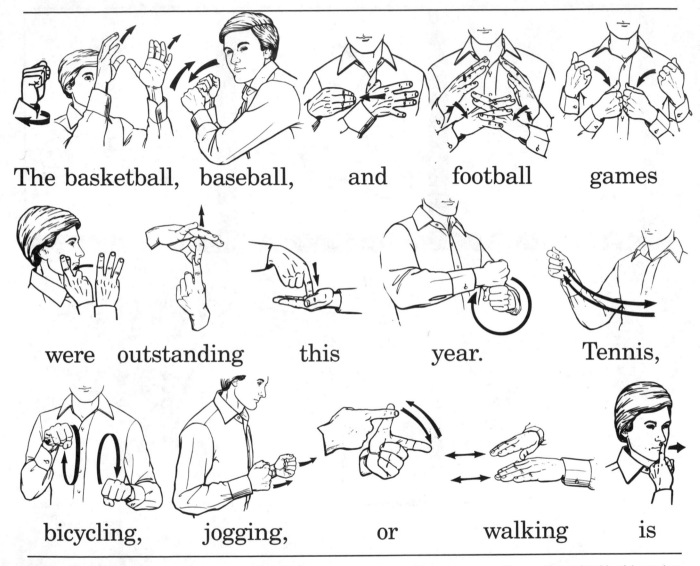

The basketball, baseball, and football games

were outstanding this year. Tennis,

bicycling, jogging, or walking is

**BASEBALL, BAT, SOFTBALL:** Place the right *S* hand above the left *S* hand and swing them forward together from the right of the body to the center of the body.

**BASKETBALL:** Hold both curved open hands at head level and move them forward and upward.

**BICYCLE, CYCLE, TRICYCLE:** Move both downturned *S* hands forward in alternate circles.

**FOOTBALL:** Interlock the fingers of both hands vigorously a few times.

**GAME, CHALLENGE:** Hold both *A* hands in front and to the sides of the chest with palms facing self. Bring the hands firmly together until the knuckles touch.

**JOGGING:** Imitate the natural back-and-forth arm movements of jogging.

**OUTSTANDING, SPECIAL, EXCEPT, EXCEPTIONAL, EXTRAORDINARY, UNIQUE:** Point the left index finger up and take hold of it with the right thumb and index finger. Raise both hands together.

**TENNIS:** Extend the right arm out to the right side with the hand closed. Move it forward across to the left and back to the right again.

**WALK, STEP:** Hold both flat hands in front with palms down; then imitate walking by moving each hand forward alternately.

**WERE:** Hold the right *W* hand slightly to the front with the palm facing left. Move it back-

ward to a position at the side of the neck or cheek while simultaneously changing from a *W* to an *R* hand.

**YEAR, LAST YEAR, NEXT YEAR:** Move the right *S* hand in a complete forward circle around the left *S* hand and come to rest with the right *S* hand on top of the left. Repeat the sign for the plural. To sign *last year*, complete the basic sign for *year*; then point the right index finger backward over the right shoulder. To sign *next year*, complete the basic sign for *year*; then point the right index finger forward.

LOOK IN INDEX FOR LOCATION OF ADDITIONAL DESCRIPTIONS.

good exercise. Grandpa listens to

the radio without his hearing aid. We

beat them. The adults won

the Ping-Pong game. Victory was not

**ADULT:** Place the right *A*-hand thumb first at the right temple, then at the right side of the chin.

**BEAT, CONQUER, DEFEAT, OVERCOME, SUBDUE:** Move the right *S* hand forward and down across the wrist of the left *S* hand.

**EXERCISE:** Hold both *S* hands up to the front with palms facing forward. Move both hands up and down (or forward and backward) simultaneously.

**GOOD, WELL:** Place the fingers of the right flat hand at the lips; then move the right hand down into the palm of the left hand.

**GRANDFATHER:** Touch the forehead with the thumb of the right open hand, and move the hand forward in two arcs.

**HEARING AID:** Place the curved fingers of the right *V* hand at the right ear. Twist a few times.

**LISTEN, HEAR:** Place the right cupped hand behind the right ear and turn the head a little to the left. *Alternative:* Point to the right ear with the right index finger.

**PING-PONG, TABLE TENNIS:** Place the right thumb tip in the crook of the right index finger with the other fingers closed. Move the hand back and forth, with most of the movement from the wrist.

**RADIO:** Cup both hands over the ears.

**THEM, THESE, THEY, THOSE:** Point the right index forward or to the persons or objects referred to, then move it to the right.

**VICTORY, CELEBRATION, CHEER, HALLELUJAH, TRIUMPH:** With tips of one or both thumbs and index fingers touching, make small circular movements. For *hallelujah*, precede sign by clapping once. For *victory*, some use *V* hands.

**WIN:** Bring both open hands together while simultaneously forming *S* hands, and place the right hand on top of the left. Hold up one or both closed hands with the tips of the thumb and index touching. Make small circular movements. *Note:* This sign is a combination of *get* and *celebration*.

LOOK IN INDEX FOR LOCATION OF ADDITIONAL DESCRIPTIONS.

expected.     Ice-skating     and     roller-skating

are     similar.     Expert     golfers

practice often.     The     last     hunting / fishing /

competition     ended     Saturday.     Everyone

**COMPETITION, CONTEST, RACE, COMPETE, RIVALRY:** Hold both *A* hands to the front with palms facing. Move them quickly back and forth alternately.

**EVERYONE, EACH, EVERY, EVERYBODY:** Hold the left *A* hand to the front with palm facing right. The knuckles and thumb of the right *A* hand rub downward on the left thumb a few times. *Note:* Add the numerical sign for *one* when signing *everyone* and *everybody*.

**EXPECT, HOPE, ANTICIPATE:** Touch the forehead with the right index finger; then bring both flat hands before the chest or head with palms facing. Bend and unbend them simultaneously a few times.

**EXPERT, COMPETENT, SHARP, SKILLFUL:** Grasp the little-finger edge of the left hand with the right hand, then move the right hand forward.

**FISHING:** Imitate holding a fishing rod.

**GOLF:** Point the right *A* hand down at waist level with the thumb side of the left *A* hand touching the little-finger side of the right hand. Swing both hands from right to left.

**HUNT, GUN, RIFLE, SHOOT:** Imitate firing a rifle.

**ICE-SKATING:** Hold both *X* hands to the front with palms facing up. Move the hands alternately forward and backward.

**LAST, END (NOUN), FINAL, LASTLY:** Hold the left hand to the front with palm

facing self and little finger extended. Strike the left little finger with the right index finger as the right hand moves down. Sometimes this sign is made with both little fingers.

**OFTEN, FREQUENT:** Place the fingertips of the right bent hand into the left palm and repeat.

**ROLLER-SKATING:** Hold both curved *V* fingers to the front with palms facing up. Move the hands alternately forward and backward.

**SIMILAR, ALIKE, SAME:** Bring index fingers together with palms facing down. *Alternative:* Move right *Y* hand back and forth if referring to self, or sideways if referring to similar persons or things.

LOOK IN INDEX FOR LOCATION OF ADDITIONAL DESCRIPTIONS.

at the party thought the movie

was boring. The group ate nuts

while playing cards. Both archery and

skiing are fun, and

---

**ARCHERY:** Imitate pulling a bow string.

**BORING, DULL, MONOTONOUS:** Touch the side of the nose with the right index finger and twist forward.

**BOTH, PAIR:** Hold the left *C* hand to the front with palm facing in. With the right palm facing in, draw the right open *V* fingers down through the left *C* hand and close the *V* fingers.

**EAT, CONSUME, DINE, FOOD, MEAL:** The right *and* hand moves toward the mouth a few times.

**FUN:** Brush the tip of the nose with the *U* fingers of the right hand, then brush them down over the left *U* fingers.

**GROUP, ASSOCIATION, AUDIENCE, COMPANY, DEPARTMENT, ORGANIZATION, SOCIETY, TEAM:** Hold both *C* hands upright before the chest with palms facing. Move the hands outward in a circle until the little fingers touch. The basic sign may be used for all the key words, but sometimes the signer will initialize the sign.

**MOVIE, CINEMA, FILM:** Place flat open hands palm to palm with the left palm facing somewhat forward. Slide the right hand back and forth over the left a few times. Most movement is from the right wrist.

**NUTS:** Move the right *A* thumb forward from behind the upper teeth.

**PARTY:** Hold both *P* hands in front and swing them back and forth from left to right.

**PLAYING CARDS:** Imitate dealing cards.

**SKIING:** Imitate the use of ski poles.

**THINK, CONSIDER, REFLECT, SPECULATE:** Make a counterclockwise circle with right index just in front of the forehead.

**WHILE, DURING, IN THE MEANTIME:** Point both index-finger hands forward with palms down and a small distance between them. Move them forward simultaneously in a slight down-forward-up curve.

LOOK IN INDEX FOR LOCATION OF ADDITIONAL DESCRIPTIONS.

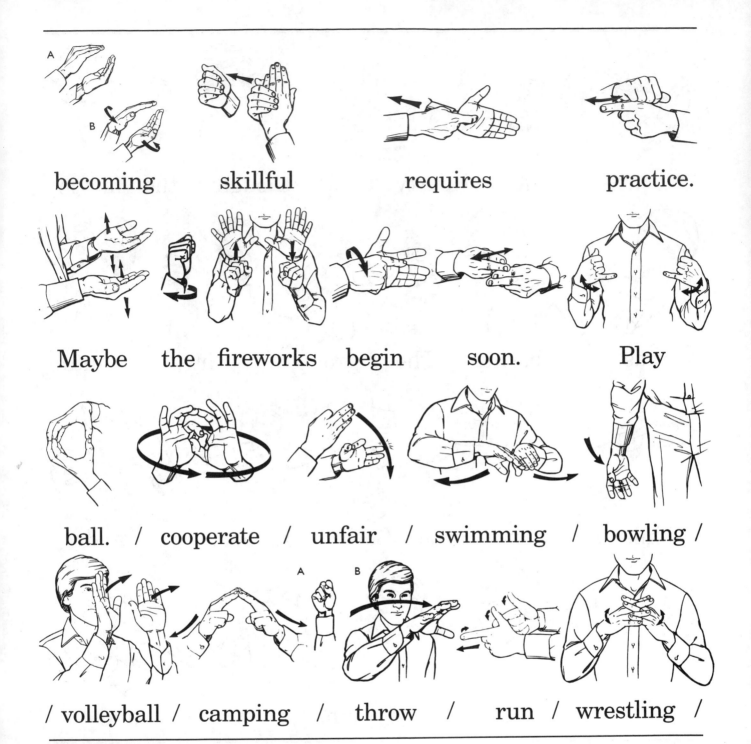

becoming　skillful　requires　practice.

Maybe　the　fireworks　begin　soon.　Play

ball. /　cooperate /　unfair /　swimming /　bowling /

/ volleyball /　camping /　throw /　run /　wrestling /

---

**BALL, ROUND, SPHERE:** Curve both hands with fingertips touching as if holding a ball. Let the thumbs and index fingers face the observer.

**BECOME, GET:** Place the curved hands in front with the right palm facing forward and the left palm facing self; then reverse positions.

**BEGIN, COMMENCE, START, INITIATE:** Hold the left flat hand forward with the palm facing right. Place the tip of the right index finger between the left index and middle fingers, then twist in a clockwise direction once or twice.

**CAMPING:** Outline tent shape with both V fingers; repeat while moving to the right.

**COOPERATE:** Interlock the index fingers and thumbs of both hands, with the other fingers extended. Move as one unit in a counterclockwise circle.

**FIREWORKS:** Raise the S hands upward alternately into open hands.

**MAYBE, MAY, PERHAPS, POSSIBLY, PROBABLY:** Hold both flat hands to front; move them up and down alternately.

**PLAY, RECREATION, ROMP:** Hold both Y hands in front of the chest and pivot them up and down a few times.

**PRACTICE, DISCIPLINE, TRAINING:** Rub the knuckles of the right A hand back and forth across the left index finger. A T hand can be used for *training*.

**REQUIRE, DEMAND, INSIST:** Thrust the bent right index finger into the left flat palm, which is facing right; then pull both hands toward the body.

**UNFAIR, UNJUST:** With palms facing, strike the fingertips of the left F hand with the fingertips of the right F hand in a downward movement.

LOOK IN INDEX FOR LOCATION OF ADDITIONAL DESCRIPTIONS.

# Practice Giving Signs

Practice signing the following sentences once again. Try to do so without referring back to the illustrations. You can also cover the page opposite if you wish.

The basketball, baseball, and football games were outstanding this year.

Tennis, bicycling, jogging, or walking is good exercise.

Grandpa listens to the radio without his hearing aid.

We beat them.

The adults won the Ping-Pong game.

Victory was not expected.

Ice-skating and roller-skating are similar.

Expert golfers practice often.

The last hunting /fishing/ competition ended last Saturday.

Everyone at the party thought the movie was boring.

The group ate nuts while playing cards.

Both archery and skiing are fun, and becoming skillful requires practice.

Maybe the fireworks begin soon.

Play ball.

/cooperate/unfair/swimming/bowling/volleyball/ camping/throw/run/wrestling/

# Fingerspelling Practice

Practice the following words at least twice with a speed that is both steady and comfortable for you.

| | | | | | |
|---|---|---|---|---|---|
| earning | agency | dignity | unable | knuckle | confuse |
| curious | preview | inside | helmsman | disagree | obscene |
| pauper | beeswax | euxenite | election | lacquer | active |
| critical | payment | disloyal | imagine | excited | phonetic |
| skyline | canary | fanciful | perilous | marina | helpless |
| incite | assistance | suitable | jumble | produce | quail |
| demerit | conclude | ghostly | rainy | nickel | enroll |

# Practice Receiving Signs

Interpret the following signs. Practicing by this method will help you receive and understand the signs more easily. Say the words out loud as you proceed.

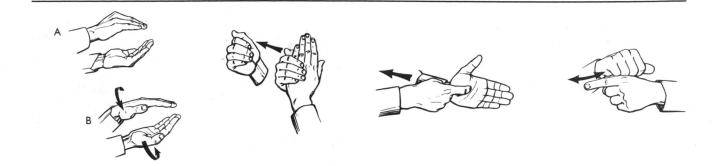

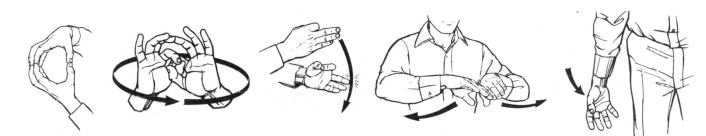

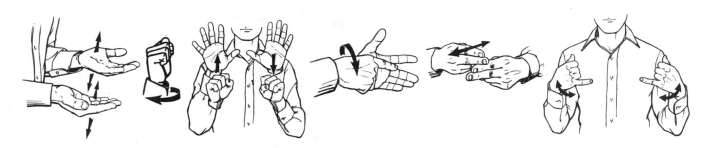

# Test Your Skill: Matching

This section uses standard matching techniques. See if you can match the signs with the words by writing the correct word next to the sign.

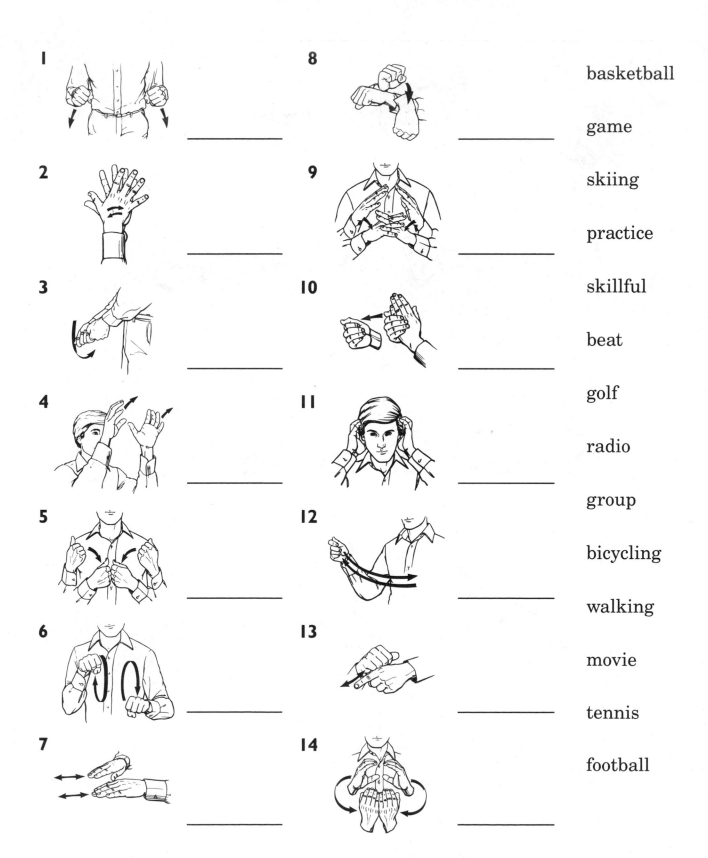

1 _____

2 _____

3 _____

4 _____

5 _____

6 _____

7 _____

8 _____

9 _____

10 _____

11 _____

12 _____

13 _____

14 _____

basketball

game

skiing

practice

skillful

beat

golf

radio

group

bicycling

walking

movie

tennis

football

# Multiple Choice

Draw a circle around or place a check mark beside the sign that matches the italicized word. For additional practice you can sign all the words in the sentences.

**1** Practice often to become an *expert* golfer.    A    B    C

**2** Everyone thought the *movie* was good.    A    B    C

**3** My *hearing aid* helps me listen to the radio.    A    B    C

**4** We went *ice-skating* for the first time on Saturday.    A    B    C

**5** The best exercise for me is *jogging*.    A    B    C

**6** Before the football *game* we went to the restaurant for pizza.    A    B    C

**7** We had a good baseball *team* this year.    A    B    C

**8** Our *skiing* trip lasted for one week.    A    B    C

# Vocabulary Review

Identify the following signs from this and previous chapters to reinforce your vocabulary.

1. _____
2. _____
3. _____
4. _____
5. _____
6. _____
7. _____
8. _____
9. _____
10. _____
11. _____
12. _____
13. _____
14. _____
15. _____
16. _____
17. _____
18. _____
19. _____
20. _____
21. _____
22. _____
23. _____
24. _____
25. _____

# Extra Practice

Sign the following sentences which contain words chosen mainly from this chapter. This will give you additional practice using the signs you have just learned.

1 Fred likes both fishing and hunting.

2 Grandpa likes the game of tennis.

3 Everyone at the party enjoyed eating the pizza.

4 The fireworks were beautiful.

5 Our parents tried ice-skating for the first time recently.

6 Let's play golf on Saturday.

7 My father goes hunting and fishing often.

8 To become skillful in archery you need much practice.

9 Grandma cannot listen to the radio without her hearing aid.

10 Our family decided to go bicycling.

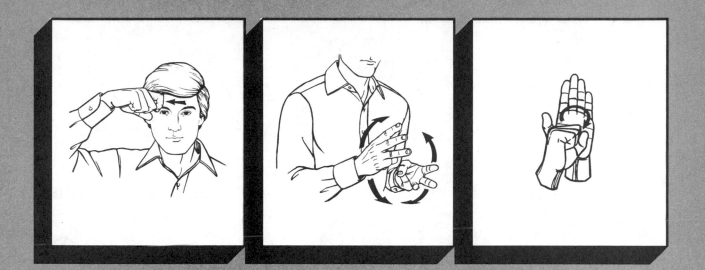

# Seasons, Time, and Weather

# Practice Learning Signs

Learn and practice the signs and sentences on each page before proceeding to the next. Descriptions are supplied at the bottom of each page.

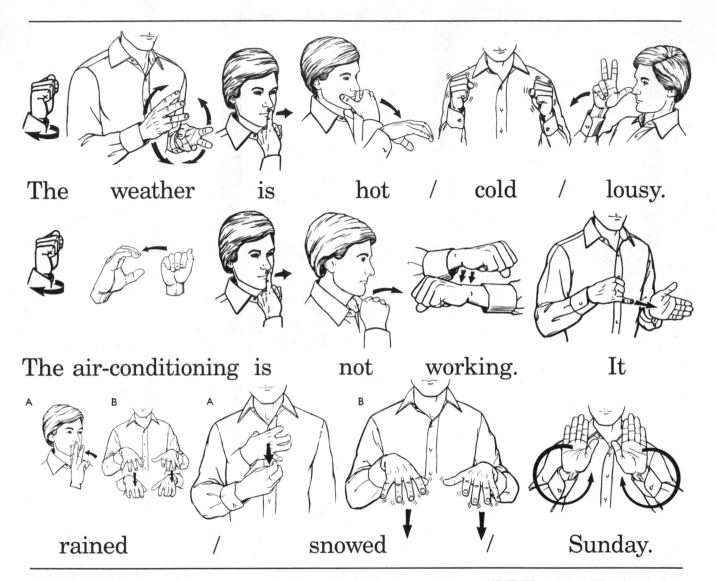

The    weather    is    hot    /    cold    /    lousy.

The air-conditioning  is    not    working.    It

A  B  A    B

rained    /    snowed    /    Sunday.

---

**AIR-CONDITIONING:** Fingerspell *A* and *C*.
**COLD, CHILLY, FRIGID, WINTER:** Hold up both *S* hands in front of the chest and shake them.
**HOT:** Place the fingers and thumb of the right *C* hand at the sides of the mouth, then quickly pivot the hand forward to the right.
**IT:** Direct the little finger of the right *I* hand into the palm of the left flat hand. Some signers prefer to fingerspell *it*.
**LOUSY, ROTTEN:** Place the thumb of the right *3* hand on the nose, then pivot the hand sharply downward. Assume an appropriate facial expression.
**RAIN:** Touch the mouth with the index finger of the right *W* hand a few times (the sign for

*water*). Move both hands down in short stages with wiggling fingers. *Note:* The first part of this sign—the sign for *water*—is not always included.
**SNOW:** Place the fingers and thumb of the right curved hand on the chest; then move it forward while simultaneously forming the *and* hand. Next move both palm-down open hands downward while simultaneously wiggling the fingers. *Note:* This is a combination of the signs for *white* and *rain*.
**SUNDAY:** Place both flat hands to the front with palms facing forward; then move them simultaneously in opposite-direction circles. The circles may be made in either direction.

**WEATHER:** Hold both *W* hands to the front with palms facing; then pivot them up and down from the wrists.
**WORKING:** The sign for *work* has been described previously, but in the sentence above it might help to clarify the meaning by adding the inflectional suffix *-ing*. See page 15 for the illustration of *-ing*.

LOOK IN INDEX FOR LOCATION OF ADDITIONAL DESCRIPTIONS.

Fall     and     winter     are     finished;

soon     warm     temperatures     will     arrive.

Spring     and     summer     are     my

favorite seasons.     A     rainbow     appeared

**APPEAR, POP UP, RISE, SHOW UP:** The right index finger is pushed up between the left index and middle fingers.
**ARRIVE, GET TO, REACH:** Move the back of the right curved hand forward into the palm of the left curved hand.
**FALL, AUTUMN:** Hold the left arm upright with a slight lean to the right. Move the right index-finger side of the right flat hand downward along the left forearm.
**FAVORITE, LUCKY:** Tap the chin a few times with the right middle finger. To sign *lucky,* touch the chin with the right middle finger; then flip the hand around so that the palm faces forward.
**FINISH, ALREADY:** Hold both open hands

to the front with palms facing self and fingers pointing up. Shake them quickly outward to the sides a few times.
**RAINBOW:** Point the fingers of the right open hand toward the mouth and wiggle them (the sign for *color*). Move the right open hand over the head from left to right in an arc.
**SEASON, AGE, EPOCH, ERA, TIME (ABSTRACT), TIMES:** For *season,* rotate the thumb side of the right *S* hand in a clockwise circle on the left flat palm. Initialize the remaining words.
**SPRING, GROW, MATURE:** Open the fingers of the right *and* hand as they pass up through the left *C* hand.

**SUMMER:** Draw the curved right index finger across the forehead from left to right.
**TEMPERATURE, FEVER, THERMOMETER:** Rub the right index finger up and down over the central part of the left upright index finger.
**WARM, HEAT:** Hold the right *A* hand in front of the mouth with palm facing in; then move it slowly upward and forward as the hand simultaneously opens.
**WINTER:** Hold up both *S* hands in front of the chest and shake them.

LOOK IN INDEX FOR LOCATION OF ADDITIONAL DESCRIPTIONS.

after the thunder - and - lightning

storm. What time is it?

See you later. Practice sign

language Monday, Tuesday, Wednesday, Thursday,

**AFTER:** Hold the left slightly curved hand out to the front with palm facing in. Place the right curved palm on the back of the left hand and move forward and away from the left hand.

**LANGUAGE, TONGUE:** Point both *L* hands toward each other (sometimes the index fingers point up), and move them to the sides with a twisting motion from the wrists.

**LATER, AFTER A WHILE, AFTERWARD, SUBSEQUENTLY:** Hold the left flat hand up with the palm facing right. Place the thumb of the right *L* hand in the center of the left palm, and pivot the right index finger forward and down.

**LIGHTNING:** Make quick jagged downward movements with the right index finger.

**MONDAY:** Make a small clockwise circle with the right *M* hand.

**PRACTICE, DISCIPLINE, TRAINING:** Rub the knuckles of the right *A* hand back and forth across the left index finger. A *T* hand can be used for *training*.

**SEE, PERCEIVE, SIGHT, VISION:** With the palm facing in, place the fingertips of the right *V* hand near eyes and move the right hand forward.

**STORM, CLOUD, GALE:** Hold both open curved hands to the front at head level with palms facing. Move both hands from one side to the other while making circular and

up-and-down movements from the wrists. Make the movement more pronounced and vigorous when signing *storm* and *gale*.

**THUNDER:** Point to the right ear with the right index finger; then move both palm-down closed hands alternately forward and backward with forceful action.

**THURSDAY:** Make a small clockwise circle with the right *H* hand. *Note:* This is sometimes signed with the manual *T* and *H,* or without rotation.

**TIME, CLOCK, WATCH:** Tap the back of the left wrist with the tip of the right curved index finger.

LOOK IN INDEX FOR LOCATION OF ADDITIONAL DESCRIPTIONS.

and    Friday.    What    is    the    day,

month,    and    year    of    her / his /

birth?    I    don't know    if    Joe

will    arrive    until    morning,    noon,

**BIRTH, BIRTHDAY, BORN:** Place the back of the right flat hand into the upturned left palm (the right hand may start from a position near the stomach). Move both hands forward and upward together. When signing *birthday,* add the sign for *day.*

**DAY, ALL DAY:** Point the left index finger to the right with palm down. Rest the right elbow on the left index finger with the right index finger pointing upward. Move the right index finger and arm in a partial arc across the body from right to left. For *all day,* hold the right index as far to the right as possible before making the arc across the body.

**DON'T KNOW, DIDN'T RECOGNIZE:** Place the fingers of the right flat hand on the forehead (the sign for *know*); then move the right hand away from the forehead with palm facing forward.

**IF:** Point the two *F* hands forward and move them up and down alternately.

**MONTH, MONTHLY:** Point the left index finger up with palm facing right. Move the right index finger from the top to the base of the left index finger. Repeat a few times to sign *monthly.*

**MORNING, FORENOON:** Place the left flat hand with palm facing the body in the bend of the right elbow. Bring the right flat hand toward self until the arm is upright with palm facing the body.

**NOON, MIDDAY:** Point the left flat hand to the right with palm facing down. Rest the right elbow on the back of the left hand with the right arm vertical and palm facing left.

**UNTIL:** Hold the left index finger up with palm facing inward. Move the right index finger in a slow forward arc until it touches the tip of the left index finger.

**YEAR, LAST YEAR, NEXT YEAR:** Move the right *S* hand in a complete forward circle around the left *S* hand and come to rest with the right *S* hand on top of the left. Repeat the sign for the plural. To sign *last year,* complete basic sign for *year;* then point the right index backward over right shoulder. To sign *next year,* complete basic sign for *year;* then point right index forward.

LOOK IN INDEX FOR LOCATION OF ADDITIONAL DESCRIPTIONS.

or　　　afternoon.　　　It　　　was　　　slippery.

We　　　waited　　　four　　　hours　　　and

twenty-two minutes　　　for　　　the　　　train.　　　Future

generations　　　will　　　forever　　　remember　　　our

**AFTERNOON:** Hold the left arm in a horizontal position pointing to the right. The left hand is flat with palm facing down. Place the right forearm on the back of the left hand at a 45-degree angle.

**FOREVER, ETERNAL, EVER, EVERLASTING:** Make a clockwise circle with the right index finger; then move the right palm-down Y hand forward.

**FUTURE, BY AND BY, LATER ON, SOMEDAY:** Hold the right flat hand with palm facing left in an upright position close to the right temple. Move it in a forward-upward arc. The greater the arc, the more distant the future that is indicated.

**GENERATION, ANCESTORS, DESCENDANTS:** Start with both slightly cupped hands at the right shoulder; then roll them one over the other in a downward-forward movement. Reverse the action if a past generation is referred to.

**HOUR:** Point the fingers of the left flat hand either up or forward with palm facing right. Move the index finger of the right D hand in a complete clockwise circle by rotating the wrist. Keep the right index finger in constant contact with the left hand.

**MINUTE, MOMENT, SECOND:** Hold the flat left hand vertically with palm facing right. Let the index finger of the right D hand

touch the left palm with the index finger pointing up. Make a short movement forward with the right index finger.

**REMEMBER, MEMORY, RECALL, RECOLLECT:** Place the thumb of the right A hand on the forehead; then place it on top of the left A-hand thumb.

**SLIDE, SLIP:** Slide the right downturned V fingers across the left flat palm.

**WAIT, PENDING:** With palms facing up, hold both curved open hands up to the left with the right hand behind the left. Wiggle all the fingers.

LOOK IN INDEX FOR LOCATION OF ADDITIONAL DESCRIPTIONS.

first     president.     The     moon     will     rise

early     tomorrow     night.     /     sun     /     ice     /

/     cool     /     warn     /     wind     /     past / time (abstract) /

/     wet     /     dry     / umbrella /     long     /     dark     /

**COOL, REFRESH:** Place both flat or open hands to the front and sides of the face with palms facing in. Simultaneously flap the fingers of both hands up and down.

**DARK, DIM:** Cross the palms of both flat hands down in front of the face.

**EARLY:** Hold the left closed hand palm down and pointing right. Touch the right middle fingertip on the back of the left hand beginning at the thumb side; then move it across the hand to the little-finger side.

**ICE, FREEZE, RIGID:** Hold both open hands to the front with palms facing down. Curve the fingers and make them rigid while simultaneously moving the hands down a short distance.

**PAST, AGO, FORMERLY, LAST, ONCE UPON A TIME, PREVIOUSLY, USED TO:** Move the right upraised flat hand backward over the right shoulder with palm facing the body. The amount of emphasis with which sign is made can vary depending on the length of time involved.

**RISE, ARISE, GET UP:** Place both flat hands to the front with palms up, and move them upward once or twice.

**SUN, SUNSHINE:** Point the right index finger forward just above head level and make a clockwise circle. To sign *sunshine,* add the action of either one or both *and* hands moving down and across the body while simultaneously forming open hands.

**TOMORROW:** Touch the right *A* thumb on the right cheek or chin area; then make a forward arc.

**WET, DRENCH, SATURATE, SOAK:** Tap the right side of the mouth with the index finger of the right *W* hand a few times. Hold both curved open hands to front with palms up, then move hands down slowly while simultaneously forming *and* hands. *Note:* This sign is a combination of *water* and *soft.*

**WIND, BLOW, BREEZE:** Hold both open hands up at head level with palms facing. Sweep them back and forth from left to right a few times.

LOOK IN INDEX FOR LOCATION OF ADDITIONAL DESCRIPTIONS.

# Practice Giving Signs

Practice signing the following sentences once again. Try to do so without referring back to the illustrations. You can also cover the page opposite if you wish.

The weather is hot /cold/lousy/.

The air-conditioning is not working.

It rained /snowed/ Sunday.

Fall and winter are finished; soon warm temperatures will arrive.

Spring and summer are my favorite seasons.

A rainbow appeared after the thunder-and-lightning storm.

What time is it?

See you later.

Practice sign language Monday, Tuesday, Wednesday, Thursday, and Friday.

What is the day, month, and year of her / his / birth?

I don't know if Joe will arrive until morning, noon, or afternoon.

It was slippery.

We waited four hours and twenty-two minutes for the train.

Future generations will forever remember our first president.

The moon will rise early tomorrow night.

/sun/ice/cool/warn/wind/past/time (abstract)/ wet/dry/umbrella/long/dark/

# Fingerspelling Practice

Practice the following words at least twice with a speed that is both steady and comfortable for you.

| | | | | | |
|---|---|---|---|---|---|
| Providence | Tampa | Shreveport | Casper | Peoria | Buffalo |
| Aberdeen | Frankfort | Waterloo | Topeka | Oakland | Lansing |
| Duluth | Utica | Danville | Springfield | Raleigh | Minneapolis |
| Sheridan | Omaha | Orlando | Amarillo | Tuscaloosa | Lincoln |
| Lubbock | Everett | Albuquerque | Durango | Paducah | Memphis |
| Beaumont | Detroit | Augusta | Milwaukee | Albany | Carlsbad |
| Richmond | Olympia | Jackson | Nashville | Hartford | Bozeman |

# Practice Receiving Signs

Interpret the following signs. Practicing by this method will help you receive and understand signs more easily. Say the words out loud as you proceed.

# Vocabulary Review

Identify the following signs from this and previous chapters to reinforce your vocabulary.

1. _____  2. _____  3. _____  4. _____  5. _____

6. _____  7. _____  8. _____  9. _____  10. _____

# Test Your Skill: Matching

This section uses standard matching techniques. See if you can match
the signs with the words by writing the correct word next to the sign.

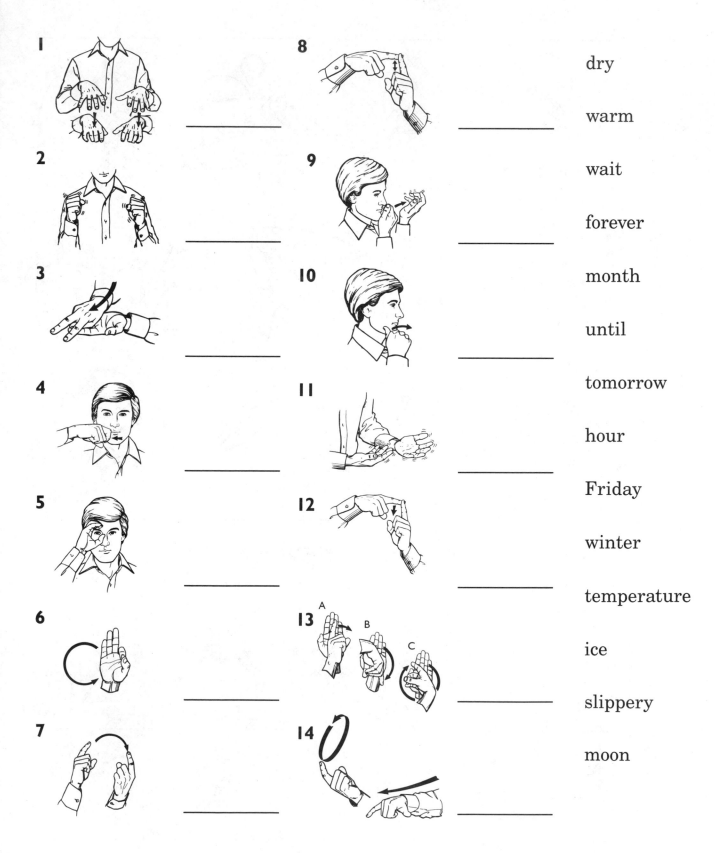

1 _____

2 _____

3 _____

4 _____

5 _____

6 _____

7 _____

8 _____

9 _____

10 _____

11 _____

12 _____

13 _____

14 _____

dry

warm

wait

forever

month

until

tomorrow

hour

Friday

winter

temperature

ice

slippery

moon

# Multiple Choice

Draw a circle around or place a check mark beside the sign that matches the italicized word. For additional practice you can sign all the words in the sentences.

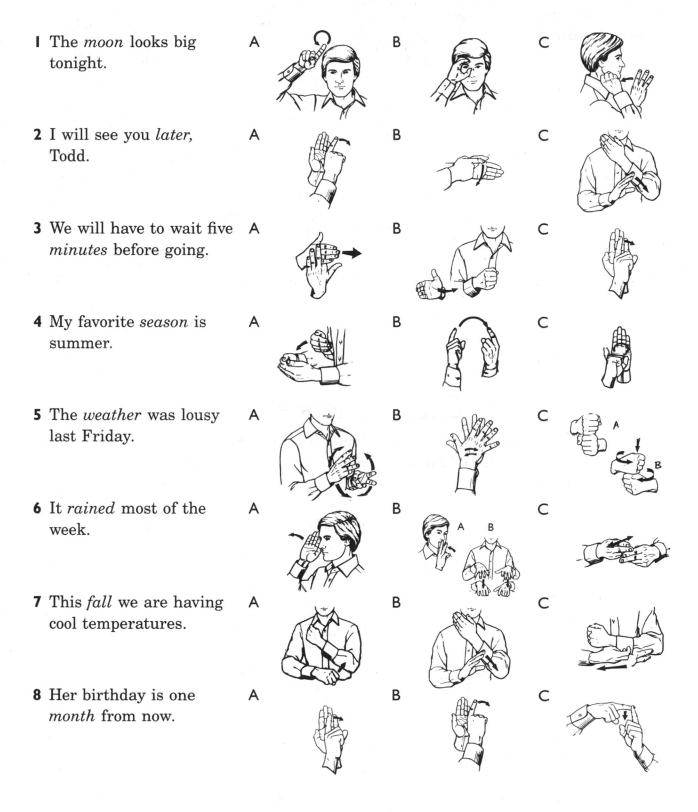

1 The *moon* looks big tonight.    A    B    C

2 I will see you *later*, Todd.    A    B    C

3 We will have to wait five *minutes* before going.    A    B    C

4 My favorite *season* is summer.    A    B    C

5 The *weather* was lousy last Friday.    A    B    C

6 It *rained* most of the week.    A    B    C

7 This *fall* we are having cool temperatures.    A    B    C

8 Her birthday is one *month* from now.    A    B    C

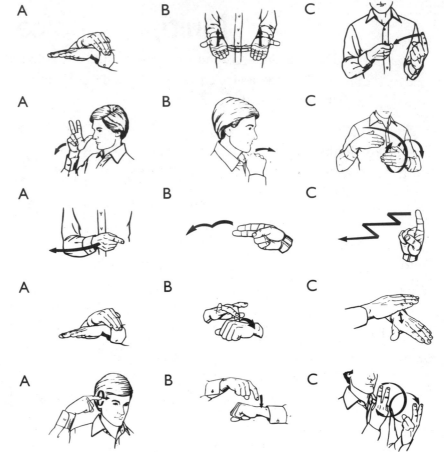

**9** We waited for the train until *night*.   A   B   C

**10** Future *generations* will forever remember George Washington.   A   B   C

**11** The thunder and *lightning* were strong today.   A   B   C

**12** Spring came *early* this year.   A   B   C

**13** What *time* on Wednesday are you leaving?   A   B   C

# Extra Practice

Sign the following sentences which contain words chosen mainly from this chapter. This will give you additional practice using the signs you have just learned.

**1** The temperature is much colder today than it was Friday.

**2** Pete will not arrive until tomorrow night.

**3** What time do you practice sign language on Wednesday?

**4** It was still raining, and the colors of the rainbow were beautiful.

**5** I don't know the year of his birth.

**6** Do you think it is hot enough to put the air conditioner on?

**7** Our president will come early in the morning.

**8** Where is my umbrella?

**9** This is a dry summer.

**10** I like walking on a windy fall day.

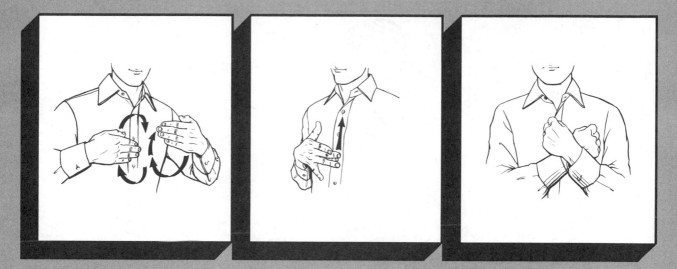

# Emotions

7

# Practice Learning Signs

Learn and practice the signs and sentences on each page before proceeding to the next. Descriptions are supplied at the bottom of each page.

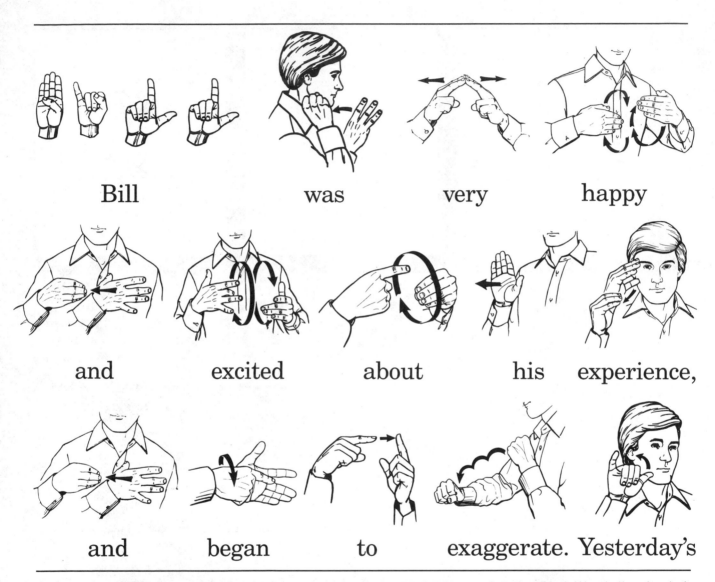

Bill     was     very     happy

and     excited     about     his     experience,

and     began     to     exaggerate. Yesterday's

**ABOUT, CONCERNING:** Move the right index finger in a forward circular direction around the fingers of the left *and* hand.

**BEGIN, COMMENCE, INITIATE, START:** Hold the left flat hand forward with the palm facing right. Place the tip of the right index finger between the left index and middle fingers, then twist in a clockwise direction once or twice.

**EXAGGERATE:** Hold the left *S* hand in front of the chest with palm facing right. Place the right *S* hand in front of the left *S* hand and move it forward while pivoting it several times from the wrist.

**EXCITE, AROUSE, STIMULATE, THRILL:** Stroke the chest a few times, using both middle fingers alternately with a forward circular motion. Extend the other fingers.

**EXPERIENCE:** Move the right curved open hand slightly outward from the right temple while simultaneously closing the hand to the *and* position.

**HAPPY, DELIGHT, GLAD, JOY, MERRY:** Move both flat hands in forward circular movements with palms touching the chest alternately or simultaneously. One hand is often used by itself.

**VERY:** With the palms facing in, touch the fingertips of both *V* hands; then draw both hands apart to the sides.

**YESTERDAY:** With the palm facing forward, place the thumb of the right *A* (or *Y*) hand on the right side of the chin. Move in a backward arc toward the ear.

LOOK IN INDEX FOR LOCATION OF ADDITIONAL DESCRIPTIONS.

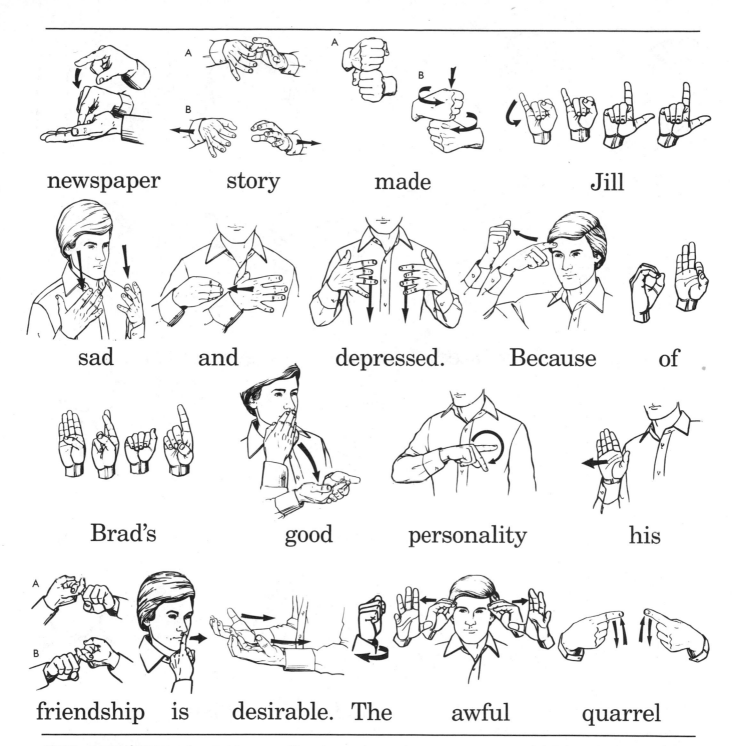

newspaper　　　　story　　　　　made　　　　　　Jill

sad　　　　and　　　　depressed.　　Because　　　　of

Brad's　　　　　good　　　　personality　　　　his

friendship　　is　　　desirable.　The　　　awful　　　quarrel

**AWFUL, CATASTROPHIC, DREADFUL, FEARFUL, HORRIBLE, TERRIBLE, TRAGIC:** Place both *O* hands near the temples and flick the fingers out while forming open hands with palms facing.

**BECAUSE:** Place the right index finger on the forehead. Move slightly to the right and upward while forming the *A* hand.

**DEPRESSED, DISCOURAGED:** Stroke the chest downward with both middle fingers simultaneously. Extend the remaining fingers.

**DESIRE, COVET, WANT:** With palms facing up, move both open curved hands toward self a few times.

**FRIENDSHIP, FRIEND:** Interlock the right and left index fingers and repeat in reverse.

**MAKE, FASHION, FIX:** Strike the right *S* hand on the top of the left *S* hand and twist the hands slightly inward. Repeat for emphasis as needed.

**NEWSPAPER, PRINTING, PUBLISHING:** Move the right index finger and thumb together as though picking something up; then place them on the left flat palm.

**PERSONALITY, ATTITUDE, CHARACTER:** Move the right *P* hand in a counterclockwise circle over the heart. To sign *attitude* and *character*, initialize the same action with an *A* and *C* hand, respectively.

**QUARREL, ROW, SQUABBLE:** Point both index fingers toward each other in front of the chest and shake them up and down from the wrists. The hands are often moved parallel to one another, but some move them up and down alternately.

**SAD, DEJECTED, DESPONDENT, DOWNCAST, FORLORN, SORROWFUL:** With palms facing in, bend the head forward slightly while dropping the open hands down the length of the face. Assume a sad expression.

**STORY, TALE:** Link the thumbs and index fingers of both *F* hands and pull them apart several times.

LOOK IN INDEX FOR LOCATION OF ADDITIONAL DESCRIPTIONS.

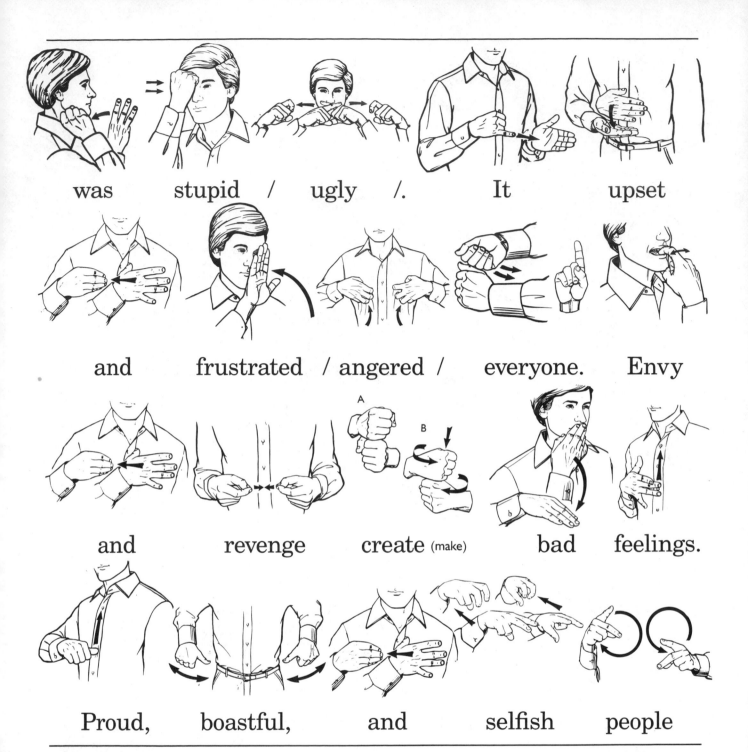

was     stupid  /  ugly  /.     It     upset

and     frustrated / angered /     everyone.     Envy

and     revenge     create (make)     bad     feelings.

Proud,     boastful,     and     selfish     people

**ANGER, FUME, RAGE, WRATH:** Place the fingertips of both curved hands against the abdomen and draw them forcefully up to the chest with slight inward curves.

**BAD:** Place the fingertips of the right flat hand at the lips; then move the right hand down and turn it so that the palm faces down.

**CREATE, MAKE:** Strike the right *S* hand on the top of the left *S* hand and twist the hands slightly inward. Repeat for emphasis as needed.

**ENVY:** Place the tip of the right index finger between the teeth and move slightly from side to side a few times.

**EVERYONE, EACH, EVERY, EVERY-**

**BODY:** Hold the left *A* hand to the front with palm facing right. The knuckles and thumb of the right *A* hand rub downward on the left thumb a few times. *Note:* Add the numerical sign for *one* when signing *everyone* and *everybody.*

**FEELING, MOTIVE, SENSATION:** Move the right middle finger upward on the chest with other fingers extended.

**FRUSTRATE:** Bring the back of the right flat hand sharply toward the face. The head can also move back slightly.

**PEOPLE:** Make inward circles alternately from the sides with both *P* hands. *Note:* Some signers prefer to direct the circles forward.

**SELFISH, GREEDY:** Pull both *V* hands toward self while simultaneously bending the *V* fingers.

**STUPID, DULL, DUMB, DUNCE:** Knock the *A* (or *S*) hand against the forehead a few times with the palm facing in.

**UGLY, HOMELY:** Cross the index fingers just below the nose with the remaining fingers closed; then bend the index fingers as the hands are pulled apart to the sides. Sometimes only one hand is used. Assume an appropriate facial expression by frowning.

**UPSET:** Place the palm of the right flat hand on the stomach; then move the hand forward and face the palm up.

LOOK IN INDEX FOR LOCATION OF ADDITIONAL DESCRIPTIONS.

always    fail.    Her    jealous

and    careless    actions / talking / gossip /

surprised    us.    Don't    be    foolish

/ crazy / lazy /    and    disappoint    me.

**ALWAYS, CONSTANTLY, EVER:** Point the right index finger forward-upward with palm up, then move it in a clockwise circle.
**CARELESS, RECKLESS, THOUGHT-LESS:** Place the right *V* hand in front of the forehead with palm facing left. Move back and forth across the forehead a few times.
**CRAZY, NUTS:** Point the right curved open hand to the temple and rotate back and forth from the wrist. *Alternative:* Point the right index finger to the temple and make a small circular movement.
**DISAPPOINT, MISS:** Place the tip of the right index finger on the chin, and assume the appropriate facial expression.
**FAIL:** Slide the back of the right *V* hand

across the upturned left hand and go be-yond and below the left fingertips.
**FOOLISH, NONSENSE, RIDICULOUS, SILLY:** Pass the right *Y* hand rapidly back and forth in front of the forehead a few times. The palm faces left.
**GOSSIP:** Open and close the *Q* fingers and thumbs several times in front of the mouth.
**JEALOUS:** Put the right little fingertip at the corner of the mouth and give it a twist.
**LAZY, SLOTHFUL:** Tap the palm of the right *L* hand at the left shoulder several times.
**SURPRISE, AMAZE, ASTONISH, AS-TOUND:** Place both closed hands at the temples with index fingertips and thumb tips

touching. Flick both index fingers up simultaneously.
**TALK, COMMUNICATE, CONVERSA-TION, DIALOGUE, INTERVIEW:** Move both index fingers back and forth from the lips alternately. Use *C* hands for *communi-cate* and *conversation, D* hands for *di-alogue,* and *I* hands for *interview.*

LOOK IN INDEX FOR LOCATION OF ADDITIONAL DESCRIPTIONS.

# Practice Giving Signs

Practice signing the following sentences once again. Try to do so without referring back to the illustrations. You can also cover the page opposite if you wish.

Bill was very happy and excited about his experience, and began to exaggerate.

Yesterday's newspaper story made Jill sad and depressed.

Because of Brad's good personality his friendship is desirable.

The awful quarrel was stupid /ugly/.

It upset and frustrated /angered/ everyone.

Envy and revenge create bad feelings.

Proud, boastful, and selfish people always fail.

Her jealous and careless actions /talking/ gossip/ surprised us.

Don't be foolish /crazy/lazy/ and disappoint me.

# Fingerspelling Practice

Practice the following words at least twice with a speed that is both steady and comfortable for you.

| | | | | | |
|---|---|---|---|---|---|
| Algeria | Bulgaria | Ecuador | Haiti | Israel | Mongolia |
| Argentina | Cambodia | Egypt | Honduras | Jamaica | Nicaragua |
| Australia | Chile | Ethiopia | Hungary | Jordan | Panama |
| Bahamas | Columbia | France | Iceland | Kuwait | Senegal |
| Barbados | Cuba | Ghana | Indonesia | Lebanon | Thailand |
| Belgium | Cyprus | Greece | Iraq | Luxemburg | Uruguay |
| Bolivia | Denmark | Guyana | Ireland | Mexico | Venezuela |

# Practice Receiving Signs

Interpret the following signs. Practicing by this method will help you receive and understand the signs more easily. Say the words out loud as you proceed.

I    will    honestly    admit:    that

drama    was    terrible.    Why    were

you    embarrassed?    We    have    nothing

to    worry    /    complain    /    about.    Please

**ADMIT, ACKNOWLEDGE, CONFESS:** Begin with the fingertips of both hands pointing down and touching the chest. Simultaneously move the hands in an upward-forward arc until they are pointing forward with palms facing up.

**COMPLAIN, GRIPE, GRUMBLE, OBJECT, PROTEST:** Strike the fingertips of the curved right hand sharply against the chest. Repeat a few times.

**DRAMA, ACT, PERFORM, PLAY, SHOW, THEATER:** Rotate both A hands inward toward the body with the palms facing each other. To sign *theater,* add the sign for *house.*

**EMBARRASS, BASHFUL, BLUSH:** Raise and lower both open hands alternately in front of the face with palms facing in. Sometimes the hands are rotated slightly forward at the same time. To sign *blush,* begin by stroking the right index finger down across the lips (the sign for *red*).

**HONEST:** Move the middle finger of the right H hand along the left upturned flat hand from palm to fingertips.

**NOTHING, NONE, NO:** Hold both O hands in front of the chest and move them to the side in opposite directions.

**TERRIBLE, AWFUL:** Place both O hands near temples and flick fingers out forming open hands with palms facing.

**WERE:** Hold the right W hand slightly to the front with the palm facing left. Move it backward to a position at the side of the neck or cheek while simultaneously changing from a W to an R hand.

**WHY:** Touch the forehead with the fingers of the right hand; then move forward while simultaneously forming the Y hand with the palm facing in.

**WORRY, ANXIOUS, FRET:** Rotate both flat or slightly curved hands in front of the head in opposite directions.

LOOK IN INDEX FOR LOCATION OF ADDITIONAL DESCRIPTIONS.

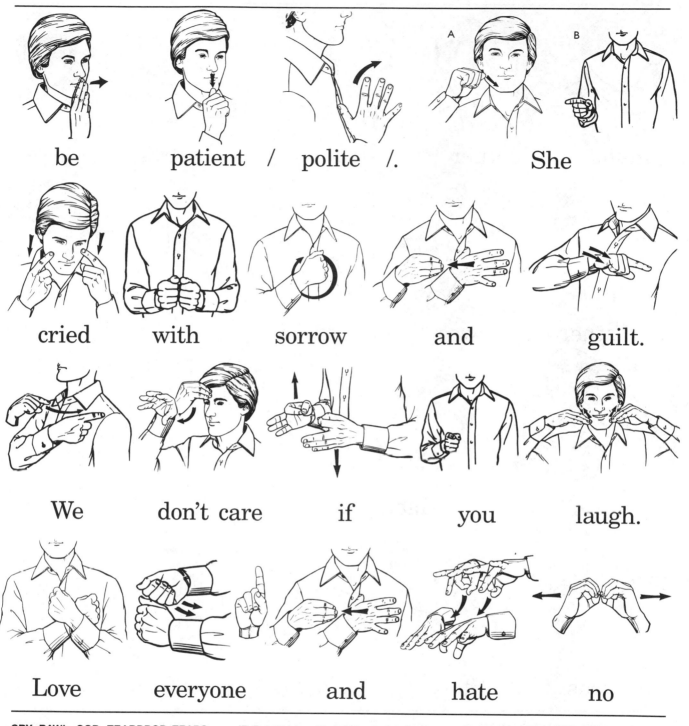

be    patient  /  polite  /.    She

cried    with    sorrow    and    guilt.

We    don't care    if    you    laugh.

Love    everyone    and    hate    no

**CRY, BAWL, SOB, TEARDROP, TEARS, WEEP:** Move one or both index fingers down the cheeks from underneath the eyes a few times.

**DON'T CARE:** Place the fingers of the closed *and* hand on the forehead; then flick the hand forward while simultaneously opening the fingers.

**GUILTY:** Tap the right G hand against the heart area a few times.

**HATE, ABHOR, DESPISE, DETEST, LOATHE:** Hold both open hands in front of the chest with palms facing down, and flick both middle fingers outward simultaneously.

**IF:** Point the two *F* hands forward and move them up and down alternately with palms facing each other.

**LAUGH, CHUCKLE, GIGGLE:** Starting near the corners of the mouth, move both index fingers upward over the cheeks a few times. Assume an appropriate facial expression.

**LOVE:** Cross either closed or flat hands over the heart with palms facing in.

**PATIENCE, BEAR:** Move the right *A* thumb downward over the lips.

**POLITE, COURTEOUS, MANNERS:** Place the thumb edge of the right flat open

hand at the chest and pivot the hand forward a few times or wiggle the fingers instead of pivoting the hand.

**SORROW, APOLOGY, REGRET:** Rotate the right *A* (or *S*) hand in a few counterclockwise circles over the heart.

LOOK IN INDEX FOR LOCATION OF ADDITIONAL DESCRIPTIONS.

man. Mother kissed the baby's face.

Father was proud of his

son's ambition. She's never

nervous. Stop teasing / confusing / me.

**AMBITION, AIM, GOAL, OBJECTIVE:** Hold the left index finger upward to the front in a position slightly higher than the head. Touch the forehead with the right index finger and move it forward and upward until it touches the tip of the left index finger.

**BABY, INFANT:** Hold the arms in the natural position for cradling a baby and rock the arms sideways.

**CONFUSE, MIX, SCRAMBLE:** Place the left curved open hand in front with palm facing up. Circle the right curved open hand in a counterclockwise direction above the left.

**FACE:** Move the right index finger in a counterclockwise direction around the face.

**KISS:** Place the fingers of the right hand on the lips and then on the cheek.

**NERVOUS, JITTERY, JUMPY:** Hold both open hands to the front with palms facing down and make the hands tremble.

**PROUD, ARROGANT, HAUGHTY:** With palm facing down, place the thumb of the right *A* hand against the chest and move straight up. The head can be raised slightly with a disdainful facial expression.

**SON:** First sign *male;* then move the right flat hand with palm facing up into the crook of the bent left elbow.

**STOP, CEASE, HALT:** Bring the little-finger side of the right flat hand down sharply at right angles on the left palm.

LOOK IN INDEX FOR LOCATION OF ADDITIONAL DESCRIPTIONS.

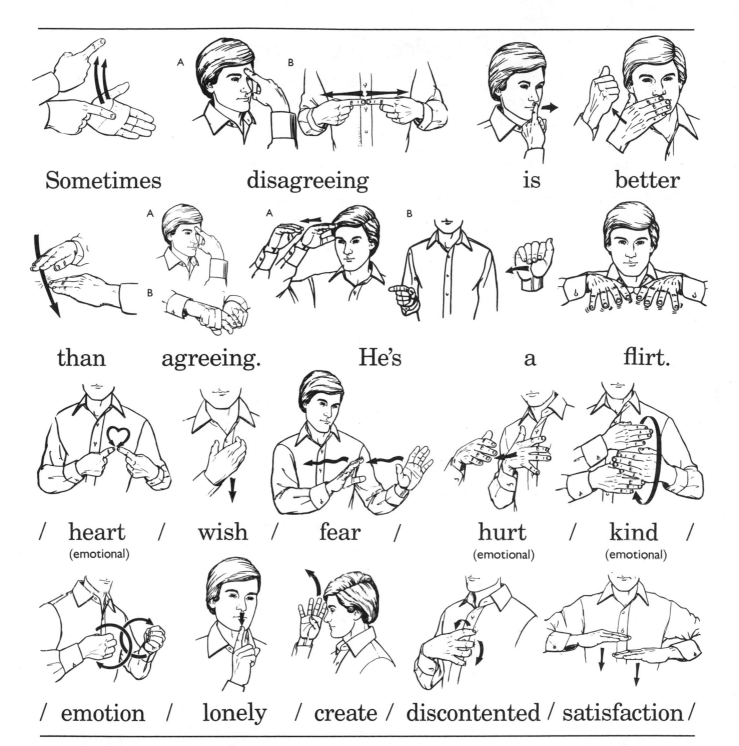

Sometimes     disagreeing              is          better

than        agreeing.        He's         a          flirt.

/ heart /     wish /    fear /       hurt /      kind /
(emotional)                              (emotional)   (emotional)

/ emotion /     lonely    / create / discontented / satisfaction /

**AGREE, ACCORD, CONSENT:** Touch the forehead with the right index finger, and then sign *same*.

**BETTER:** Touch the lips with the fingers of the right flat hand; then move it to the right side of the head while forming an *A* hand.

**CREATE, INVENT, MAKE UP:** Push the index finger of the right *4* hand upward on the forehead with a slight forward curve.

**DISAGREE, CONTRADICT, CONTRARY TO, DIFFER:** Touch the forehead with the right index finger; then touch the fingertips of both *D* index fingers and pull them away from each other sharply.

**DISCONTENTED, DISGUSTED, DISPLEASING, DISSATISFIED:** Touch the chest with the thumb and fingertips of the right open curved hand; then rock the hand back-and-forth in a circular movement.

**EMOTION:** Stroke the chest alternately with both *E* hands moving in forward circles.

**FEAR, DREAD, TERROR:** Hold both open hands to the front with palms facing forward; then draw them in and down toward the body with a trembling motion. Assume an appropriate facial expression.

**FLIRT, PHILANDERER:** Touch the thumbs of the palm-down open hands and wiggle the fingers.

**HURT (EMOTION):** Place the right middle finger over the heart with other fingers extended; then twist the hand quickly forward and outward from the wrist.

**KIND (EMOTION), BENEVOLENT, GENTLE, GRACIOUS:** Place the right flat hand over the heart; then circle it around the left flat hand which is held a short distance from the chest with palm facing in.

**SATISFACTION, CONTENT:** Move both flat hands downward in front of the chest with the right hand slightly above the left. *Alternative:* With hands in same position bring them in to touch the chest.

**THAN:** Hold the left flat or curved hand to the front with palm facing down. Brush the index-finger edge of the right flat hand down off the fingertips of the left hand.

LOOK IN INDEX FOR LOCATION OF ADDITIONAL DESCRIPTIONS.

# Practice Giving Signs

Practice signing the following sentences once again. Try to do so without referring back to the illustrations. You can also cover the page opposite if you wish.

I will honestly admit: that drama was terrible.

Why were you embarrassed?

We have nothing to worry /complain/ about.

Please be patient /polite/.

She cried with sorrow and guilt.

We don't care if you laugh.

Love everyone and hate no man.

Mother kissed the baby's face.

Father was proud of his son's ambition.

She's never nervous.

Stop teasing /confusing/ me.

Sometimes disagreeing is better than agreeing.

He's a flirt.

/heart (emotional)/wish/fear/hurt (emotional)/ kind (emotional)/emotion/lonely/create/ discontented/satisfaction/

# Vocabulary Review

Identify the following signs from this and previous chapters to reinforce your vocabulary.

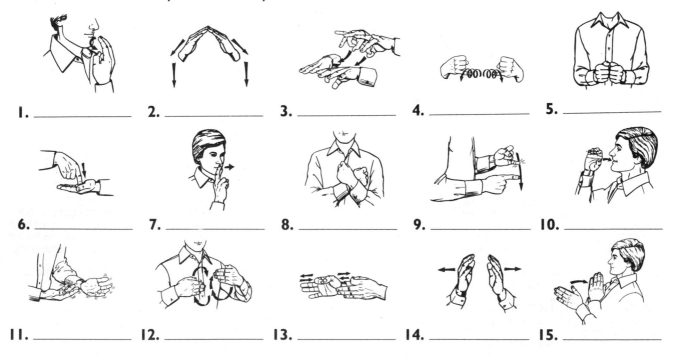

1. _____   2. _____   3. _____   4. _____   5. _____

6. _____   7. _____   8. _____   9. _____   10. _____

11. _____   12. _____   13. _____   14. _____   15. _____

# Fill In the Blanks

Sign the following sentences and choose an appropriate sign for the blank spaces. Use the skill you have gained thus far to complete the sentences logically. There may be more than one answer for each blank space. The first one is already completed as an example for you.

1. Don't <u>embarrass</u> me by being boastful.

2. Eugene was very _____ and excited about the _____ newspaper story.

3. The mother was _____ that her son was _____.

4. Please be _____ and don't worry.

5. Don't complain when your father _____ about his experiences.

6. She was depressed and would not _____ to anyone.

7. I was frustrated and _____ with my _____ attitude.

8. Her _____ ruined their friendship.

9. I appreciate your being _____ to my sister.

10. Don't let _____ keep you from success.

11. Have a _____ time and _____ as much as you want.

12. The _____ quarrel _____ everyone.

13. It is much better to _____ than to _____.

14. She was _____ about her new job.

15. He is a _____ person.

16. I am _____ you are not a _____ person.

17. We are _____ he is feeling so _____.

18. It was _____ meeting her mother for the first time.

19. I wish you would be _____ to me.

20. Be _____ and admit that you are lonely.

# Extra Practice

Sign the following sentences which contain words chosen mainly from this chapter. This will give you additional practice using the signs you have just learned.

1 We agreed not to gossip about the problem.

2 He has a proud and boastful personality.

3 We were surprised at Lee's patience.

4 My son's ambition made me happy.

5 I was very pleased and satisfied with the drama.

6 He was a kind friend and liked by everyone.

7 Stop teasing and embarrassing me.

8 Don't do something foolish because you are discontented.

9 I wish you wouldn't laugh at me.

10 He disagrees with everything I say.

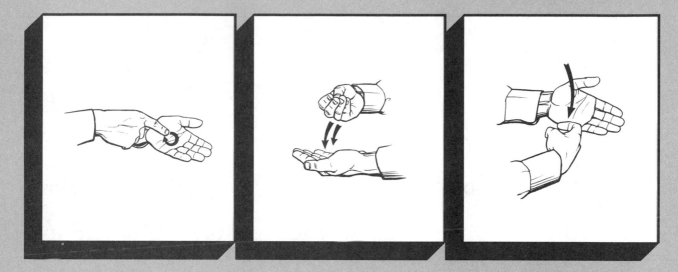

# Money
# and
# Shopping

8

# Practice Learning Signs

Learn and practice the signs and sentences on each page before proceeding to the next. Descriptions are supplied at the bottom of each page.

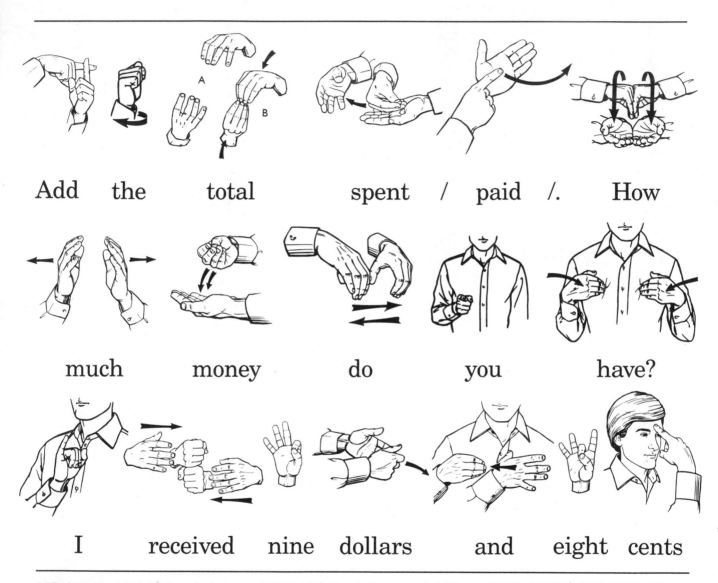

Add     the     total     spent     /     paid     /.     How

much     money     do     you     have?

I     received     nine     dollars     and     eight     cents

**ADD:** Cross the right index finger horizontally over the left vertical index finger.
**CENTS:** Touch the forehead with the right index finger and then sign the appropriate number.
**DOLLARS, BILLS:** Point the fingers of the left flat hand to the right. Grasp the left fingers between the right palm and fingers (or thumb and fingers), then pull the right hand away from the left a few times.
**EIGHT:** See "Numbers" on page 15.
**MONEY, CAPITAL, FINANCES, FUNDS:** Strike the back of the right *and* hand into the left upturned palm a few times.

**MUCH, LOT:** Place both open and slightly curved hands to the front with palms facing; then draw them apart to the sides.
**NINE:** See "Numbers" on page 15.
**PAY:** Hold the left flat hand to the front with palm facing up. Place the tip of the right index finger into the left palm and swing it forward until the index finger points away from the body.
**SPEND, SQUANDER, WASTE:** Bring the back of the right *and* hand down into the left upturned palm. Open the right hand as it slides off the fingertips of the left hand.

**TOTAL, AMOUNT, SUM:** Hold the left open curved hand over the right open curved hand with palms facing. Bring the hands together while simultaneously forming *and* hands until the fingertips touch.

LOOK IN INDEX FOR LOCATION OF ADDITIONAL DESCRIPTIONS.

138

in    change.    Stores    usually    make

big    profits    during    holidays.    Dan

recently    decided    to    buy    a

coat,    gloves,    hat,    shirt,    shoes,

**BIG, ENORMOUS, GREAT, HUGE, IMMENSE, LARGE:** Hold both *L* hands to the front with palms facing. Move them outward to the sides beyond the width of the body.
**BUY, PURCHASE:** Move the back of the right *and* hand down into the upturned palm of the left hand, then up and straight out or slightly to the right.
**CHANGE, COINS:** Make a small circle on the left flat palm with the right index finger.
**COAT, JACKET, OVERCOAT:** Move the thumbs of both *A* hands downward from either side of the base of the neck to the center of the lower chest.
**DURING, IN THE MEANTIME, WHILE:** Point both index-finger hands forward with palms down and a small distance between them. Move them forward simultaneously in a slight down-forward-up curve.
**GLOVES:** Hold the left open hand up with palm facing self. Move the right curved hand down over the back of the left hand a few times. *Alternative:* With the palms of both open and slightly curved hands facing down, move the right hand backward over the left; then the left hand backward over the right.
**HOLIDAY, LEISURE, VACATION:** Place both thumbs at the armpits and wiggle all the fingers.
**RECENTLY, JUST NOW, LATELY, A SHORT TIME AGO, A WHILE AGO:** Place the right curved index finger against the right cheek with the palm and index finger facing back. Move the index finger up and down a few times.
**SHIRT, BLOUSE:** Make a downward arc with the right flat hand from the upper to the lower chest.
**SHOES:** Strike the thumb sides of both closed hands together a few times.
**USUALLY, USED TO:** Point the fingers of the right *U* hand upward. Place the right wrist on the wrist of the left downturned closed hand; then push both hands down slightly.

LOOK IN INDEX FOR LOCATION OF ADDITIONAL DESCRIPTIONS.

and　　socks.　Borrowing　/　loaning　/　money

can　　be　a　mistake.　Many　　people

in　　America　save　/　collect　/　gold

and　　silver.　Sign　the　paper.　I

**AMERICA:** Interlock the fingers of both slightly curved open hands and move them from right to left in an outward circle.

**BORROW:** Cross the *V* hands at the wrists (the sign for *keep*) and move them toward the body.

**CAN, ABILITY, ABLE, CAPABLE, COMPETENT, COULD, POSSIBLE:** Hold both *S* (or *A*) hands to the front and move them down firmly together.

**COLLECT, EARN, SALARY, WAGES:** Sweep the curved right hand across the left palm-up flat hand, and end with the right hand closed.

**LEND, LOAN:** Cross the *V* hands at the wrists (the sign for *keep*) and move them away from the body.

**MANY, LOTS, NUMEROUS, PLURAL, SCORES:** Hold both *S* hands to the front with palms facing up. Flick the fingers and thumbs open with an upward movement. Repeat.

**MISTAKE, ERROR, FAULT, WRONG:** Place the *Y* hand on the chin with the palm facing in.

**MONEY, CAPITAL, FINANCES, FUNDS:** Strike the back of the right *and* hand into the left upturned palm a few times.

**PAPER:** Strike the left palm heel with the right palm heel a few times as the right hand moves from right to left.

**SAVE, ECONOMIZE, STORE:** Place the right *V* fingers on the back of the closed left hand with both palms facing in.

**SIGNATURE, REGISTER:** Slap the right *H* fingers down onto the left upturned palm.

**SILVER:** Touch the right ear with the right index finger. Move the right hand forward to an *S* position and shake it.

**SOCKS, HOSE, STOCKINGS:** Point both index fingers down. Rub them up and down against each other alternately.

LOOK IN INDEX FOR LOCATION OF ADDITIONAL DESCRIPTIONS.

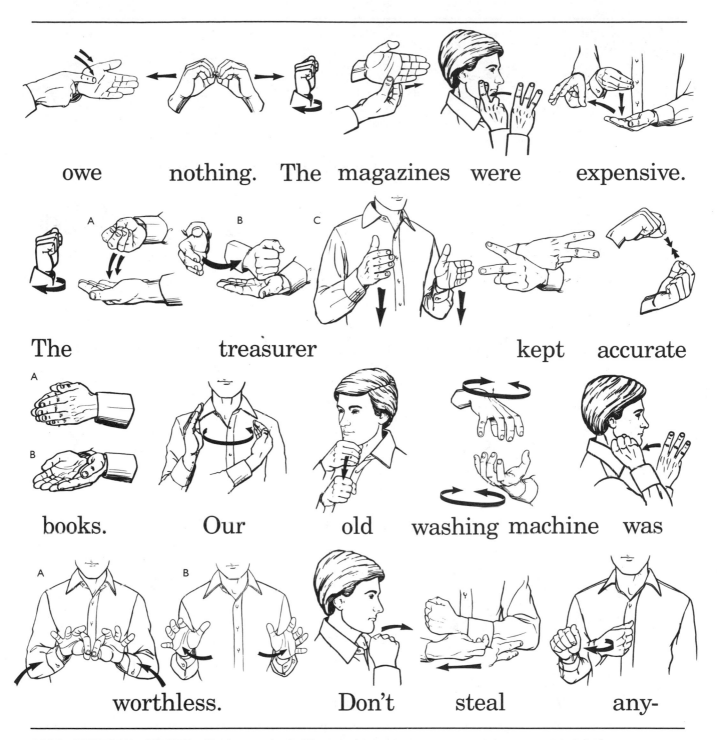

owe nothing. The magazines were expensive.

The treasurer kept accurate

books. Our old washing machine was

worthless. Don't steal any-

**BOOK, TEXTBOOK, VOLUME:** Place hands palm to palm, with fingers pointing forward. Open hands to palm-up position. Keep contact with the little fingers.

**EXPENSIVE, COSTLY:** Slap the back of the right *and* hand in the upturned palm of the left hand (the sign for *money*); then lift the right hand and open it while simultaneously pivoting it to the right.

**KEEP:** Cross the wrist of the right *V* hand over the wrist of the left *V* hand.

**MAGAZINE, BOOKLET, BROCHURE, CATALOG, LEAFLET, MANUAL, PAMPHLET:** Move the right thumb and index finger along the little-finger edge of the right flat hand. The direction of this movement varies in different locations.

**NOTHING, NONE, NO:** Hold both *O* hands in front of the chest and move them to the side in opposite directions. To sign *nothing,* keep hands open while moving to the side.

**OLD, AGE, ANCIENT, ANTIQUE:** Close the right hand just below the chin and move it downward.

**OWE, DEBT, DUE:** Tap the left palm with the right index finger several times.

**STEAL, EMBEZZLE:** Slide the curved fingers of the right *V* hand along the left forearm from the elbow to wrist. Curve the right *V* fingers even more during the action.

**TREASURER:** Bring the back of the *and* hand down onto the palm of the left flat hand

a few times. Make a scooping movement with the right hand from the fingertips to the heel of the left flat hand. Finally, bring both flat hands down simultaneously with palms facing. This is a combination of *money, collection,* and *person* (personalizing word ending).

**WASHING MACHINE:** Hold both curved open hands with palms facing each other vertically. Make twisting circular motions with hands rotating in opposite directions.

**WORTHLESS, USELESS:** Bring both *F* hands up from the sides to the center until the thumbs and index fingers touch. Swing the hands away to the sides while simultaneously forming open hands.

LOOK IN INDEX FOR LOCATION OF ADDITIONAL DESCRIPTIONS.

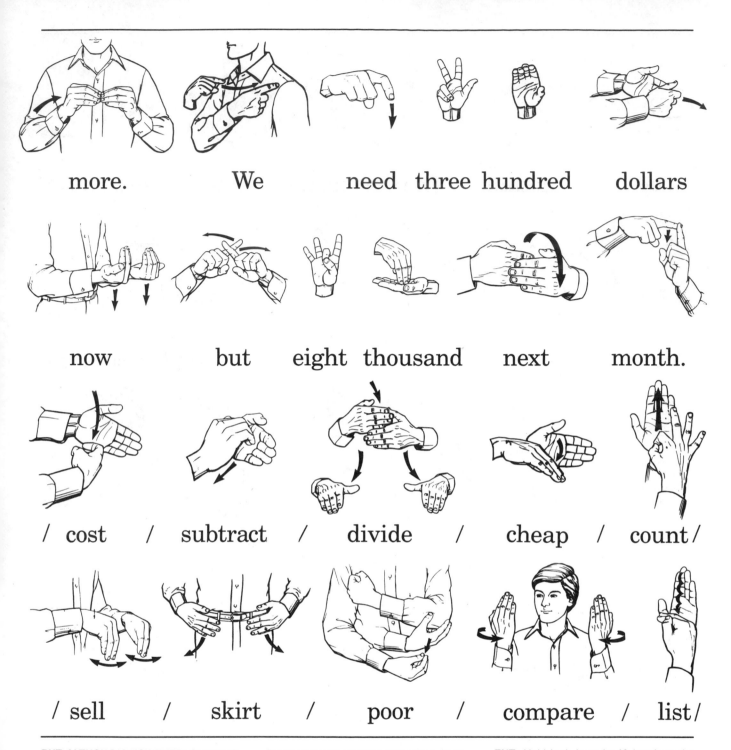

more. We need three hundred dollars

now but eight thousand next month.

/ cost / subtract / divide / cheap / count /

/ sell / skirt / poor / compare / list /

**BUT, ALTHOUGH, HOWEVER:** Cross both index fingers with palms facing out; then draw them apart a short distance.

**CHEAP, INEXPENSIVE:** Hold the left flat hand with fingers pointing forward and palm facing right. Brush the index-finger side of the slightly curved right hand downward across the palm of the left hand.

**COMPARE, CONTRAST:** With palms facing each other, hold both curved hands up near the head; then rotate the hands with an inward twist from the wrists so that both palms face the head.

**COST, CHARGE, EXPENSE, FEE, FINE, PRICE, TAX:** Strike the right crooked index

finger against the left flat palm with a downward movement.

**COUNT:** Hold up the left flat hand with the palm facing right. Move the thumb and index finger of the right *F* hand upward over the left hand from wrist to fingertips.

**DIVIDE:** Cross the little-finger edge of the right flat hand over the index-finger edge of the left flat hand. Move both hands down and to the sides with the palms facing down.

**MORE:** Touch the fingertips of both *and* hands before the chest with palms facing down. The right hand can be brought up to meet the left from a slightly lower position.

**NOW, CURRENT, IMMEDIATE, PRES-**

**ENT:** Hold both bent (or *Y*) hands to the front at waist level with palms facing up. Drop both hands sharply a short distance.

**POOR, POVERTY:** Place the right curved hand under the left elbow and pull the fingers and thumb down into the *and* position a few times.

**SKIRT:** Brush the fingers of both flat open hands downward and outward just below the waist.

**SUBTRACT, ABORTION, DEDUCT, DELETE, ELIMINATE, REMOVE:** Move the bent fingers of the right hand downward across the left flat palm.

LOOK IN INDEX FOR LOCATION OF ADDITIONAL DESCRIPTIONS.

# Practice Giving Signs

Practice signing the following sentences once again. Try to do so without referring back to the illustrations. You can also cover the page opposite if you wish.

Add the total spent.

How much money do you have?

I received nine dollars and eight cents in change.

Stores usually make big profits during holidays.

Dan recently decided to buy a coat, gloves, hat, shirt, shoes, and socks.

Borrowing /loaning/ money can be a mistake.

Many people in America save /collect/ gold and silver.

Sign the paper.

I owe nothing.

The magazines were expensive.

The treasurer kept accurate books.

Our old washing machine was worthless.

Don't steal anymore.

We need three hundred dollars now, but eight thousand next month.

/cost/subtract/divide/cheap/count/sell/skirt/ poor/compare/list/

# Fingerspelling Practice

Practice the following words at least twice with a speed that is both steady and comfortable for you.

| | | | | | |
|---|---|---|---|---|---|
| Vermilion | Lawrence | Carroll | Campbell | Wayne | Pierce |
| Logan | Marion | Kendall | Goshen | Mercer | Nelson |
| Mason | Jackson | Garfield | Johnson | Lewis | Loudoun |
| Fulton | Union | Latmer | Fremont | Spokane | Augusta |
| Douglas | Monroe | Jefferson | Webster | Okanogan | Patrick |
| Christian | Hancock | Tillman | Braxton | Cowlitz | Halifax |
| Jasper | Peoria | Beckham | Tucker | Whitman | Middlesex |

# Practice Receiving Signs

Interpret the following signs. Practicing by this method will help you receive and understand the signs more easily. Say the words out loud as you proceed.

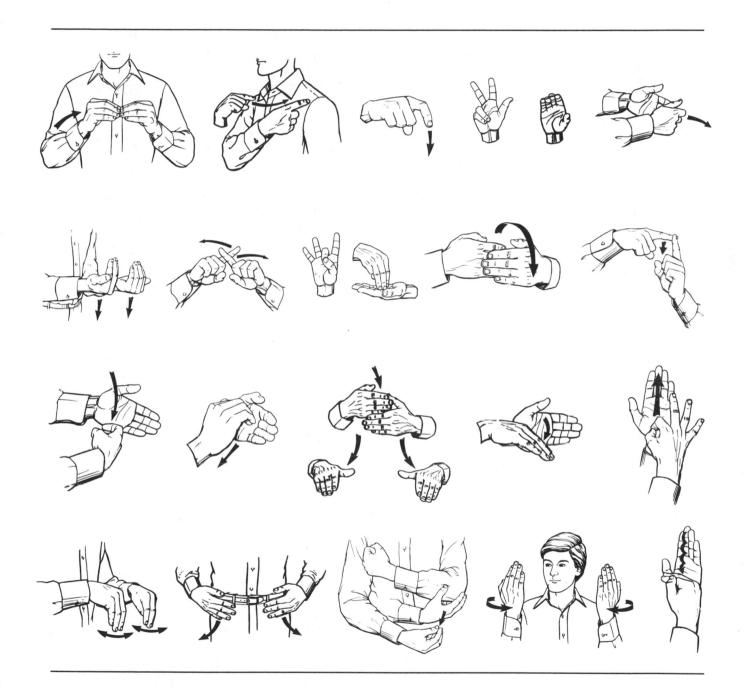

# Test Your Skill: Matching

This section uses standard matching techniques. See if you can match the signs with the words by writing the correct word next to the sign.

1 _____

2 _____

3 _____

4 _____

5 _____

6 _____

7 _____

8 _____

9 _____

10 _____

11 _____

12 _____

13 _____

14 _____

hat

money

profit

cost

borrow

buy

save

silver

store

loan

expensive

socks

shirt

worthless

**15**  _____

**16**  _____

**17**  _____

**18**  _____

**19**   _____

**20**  _____

**21**  _____

**22** _____

**23** 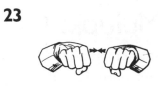 _____

**24** _____

**25**  _____

**26** _____

**27** _____

**28** _____

**29** _____

**30** _____

cheap

collect

sell

compare

skirt

mistake

count

sign (signature)

owe

list

decide

subtract

pay

shoes

steal

dollars

# Multiple Choice

Draw a circle around or place a check mark beside the sign that matches the italicized word. For additional practice you can sign all the words in the sentences.

1 How much *money* do you need?

2 We will *divide* one thousand dollars again next month.

3 Many people save *gold* in America.

4 I want to buy a *new* washing machine.

5 How much did you *spend*?

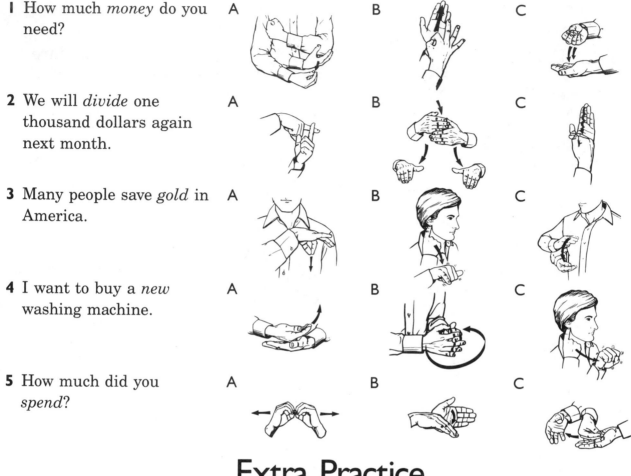

# Extra Practice

Sign the following sentences which contain words chosen mainly from this chapter. This will give you additional practice using the signs you have just learned.

1 Jan decided to buy a skirt, a coat, and shoes.

2 How much money did you spend at the store?

3 I think this washing machine is too expensive.

4 Most of the magazines were old and worthless.

5 Maybe the three hundred dollars was stolen.

6 The treasurer explained his books easily.

7 Do you think our business will be profitable this year?

8 Many people borrowed money from the bank recently.

9 Please sign the paper before tomorrow night.

10 Save your dollars and don't buy anything expensive.

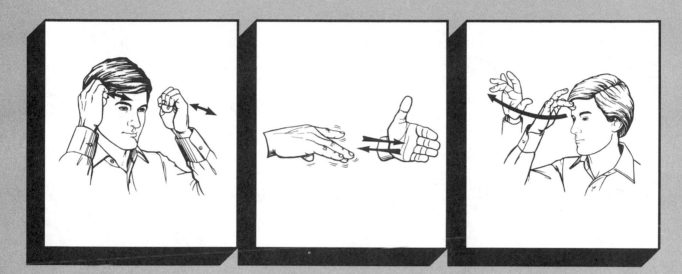

# Education

9

# Practice Learning Signs

Learn and practice the signs and sentences on each page before proceeding to the next. Descriptions are supplied at the bottom of each page.

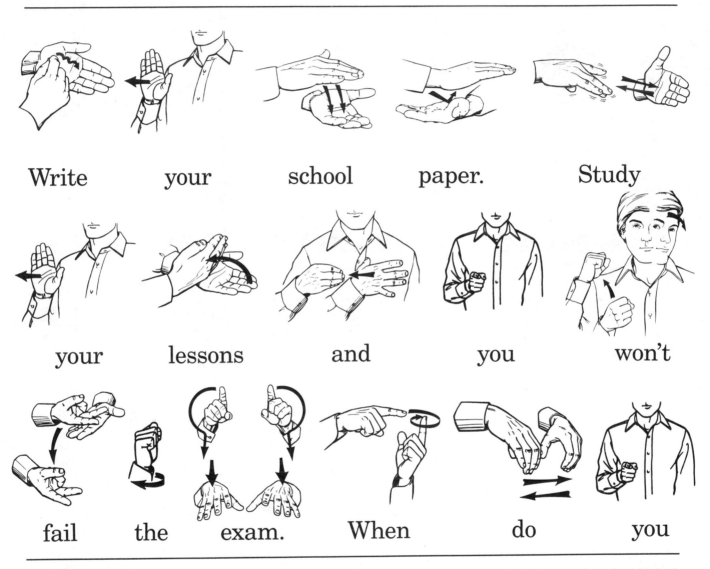

Write          your          school          paper.          Study

your          lessons          and          you          won't

fail          the          exam.          When          do          you

**EXAMINATION, QUIZ, TEST:** Hold both index fingers up and draw the shape of question marks in opposite directions, then open both hands and move them forward.
**FAIL:** Slide the back of the right *V* hand across the left upturned hand and go beyond and below the left fingertips.
**LESSON, EXERCISE (MENTAL):** Place the little-finger edge of the right flat hand across the fingers of the left flat hand. Move the right hand in a small arc so that it rests at the base of the left hand.
**PAPER:** Strike the heel of the left upturned palm two glancing blows with the heel of the right downturned palm. The right hand

moves from right to left to perform the movement.
**SCHOOL:** Clap the hands two or three times.
**STUDY:** Point the right open fingers toward the left flat hand. Move the right hand back and forth a short distance from the left while simultaneously wiggling the right fingers.
**WHEN:** Make a clockwise circle around the left index finger with the right index finger. End with the right index fingertip touching the left index fingertip. The left hand can have the palm facing to the right or upward.
**WON'T, REFUSE:** Hold the right *S* (or *A*) hand in a natural position to the front; then

move it sharply upward over the right shoulder while simultaneously turning the head to the left.
**WRITE:** Touch the right index finger and thumb with the other fingers closed; then move the right hand horizontally across the flat left palm with a slight wavy motion.

LOOK IN INDEX FOR LOCATION OF ADDITIONAL DESCRIPTIONS.

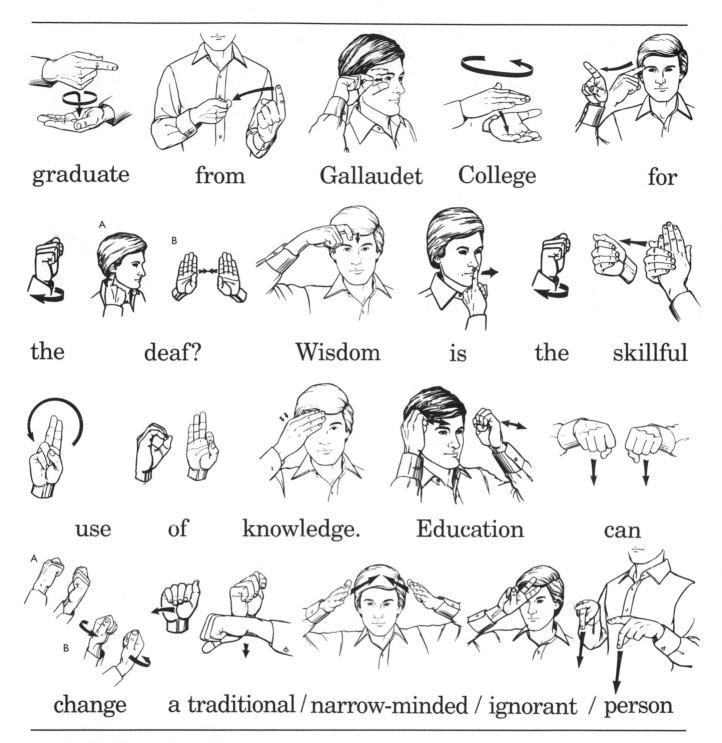

graduate    from    Gallaudet    College    for

the    deaf?    Wisdom    is    the    skillful

use    of    knowledge.    Education    can

change    a traditional / narrow-minded / ignorant / person

---

**CHANGE, ADAPT, ADJUST, ALTER:**
Place the thumb tips of both closed hands into the crook of the bent index fingers (or use *A* hands). With palms facing and hands close or touching, reverse positions.
**COLLEGE:** Place the right flat palm on the left upturned flat palm, then make a counterclockwise circle with the right hand above the left.
**DEAF:** Touch or point to the right ear with the right index finger. Place both downturned flat hands to the front and draw them together until the index fingers and thumbs touch. This last movement is the sign for *closed.*
**EDUCATION:** Move both *E* hands in and

out from the forehead a few times. *Note:* The signs for *teach* and *learn* can also be used.
**FROM:** Touch the upright left index finger with the knuckle of the right *X* index finger; then move the right hand in a slight backward-downward arc. *Note:* Sometimes the left index finger is crooked or pointed forward.
**GALLAUDET (COLLEGE), GLASSES:** Place the fingers and thumb of the right *G* hand above and below the right eye at the side. Move the fingers back to the ear while closing them.
**GRADUATE:** Make a small clockwise circle

with the right *G* hand and bring it down onto the left flat palm.
**KNOWLEDGE, INTELLIGENCE, KNOW, RECOGNIZE:** Tap the fingers of the slightly bent right hand on the forehead a few times.
**NARROW-MINDED:** Draw a *V* shape in front of the forehead.
**PERSON:** Move both *P* hands down together.
**TRADITION:** Place right *T* hand on closed left hand and lower both hands slightly.
**WISDOM, INTELLECTUAL, WISE:** Move the right bent finger of the *X* hand up and down slightly just in front of the forehead. Make the movement from the wrist.

LOOK IN INDEX FOR LOCATION OF ADDITIONAL DESCRIPTIONS.

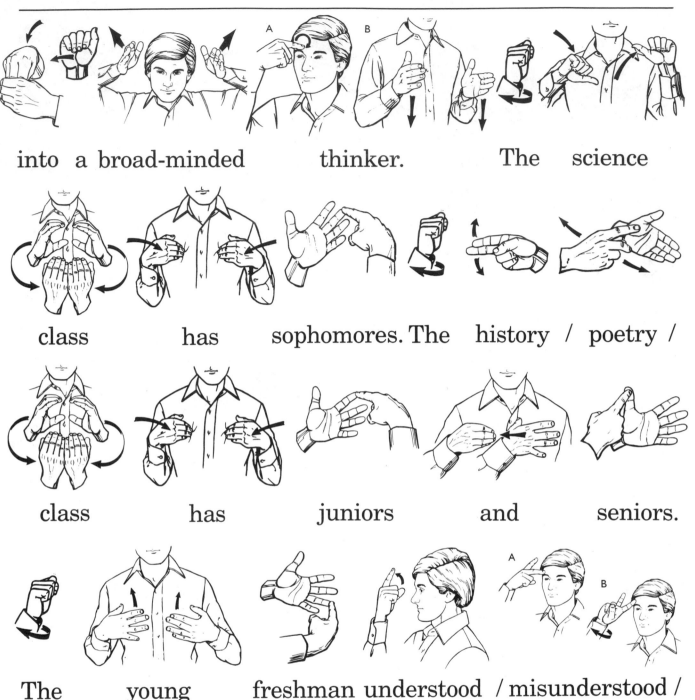

into a broad-minded thinker. The science

class has sophomores. The history / poetry /

class has juniors and seniors.

The young freshman understood / misunderstood /

**BROAD-MINDED, OPEN-MINDED:** Position both flat hands forward with palms facing each other just in front of the forehead. Move the hands forward and outward with a widening *V* shape.

**CLASS:** Move both *C* hands in outward circles from the chest until the little fingers touch.

**FRESHMAN:** Touch the fourth finger of the open left hand with the right index finger.

**HISTORY:** Shake the right *H* hand up and down a short distance.

**JUNIOR:** Touch the index finger of the left open hand with the right index finger.

**MISUNDERSTAND:** Put the right *V* hand to the forehead, touching first with one finger, then twisting the hand and touching with the other finger. Either finger may begin the sign, although many start with the index finger.

**POETRY, POEM:** Move the right *P* hand back and forth with rhythm in front of the left flat hand.

**SCIENCE, BIOLOGY, CHEMISTRY, EXPERIMENT:** Place both *A* hands in front of the shoulders and move them alternately in and down a few times. Use the appropriate initialized hands for *biology, chemistry,* and *experiment.*

**SENIOR:** Touch the thumb of the open left hand with the right index finger.

**SOPHOMORE:** Touch the middle finger of the open left hand with the right index finger.

**THINK, CONSIDER, REFLECT, SPECULATE:** Make a counterclockwise circle with the right index finger just in front of the forehead.

**UNDERSTAND, COMPREHEND:** With the palm facing in, flick the right index finger up vertically in front of the forehead.

**YOUNG, ADOLESCENT, YOUTH:** Place the fingertips of both curved hands on the upper chest and quickly pivot them upward from the wrists several times.

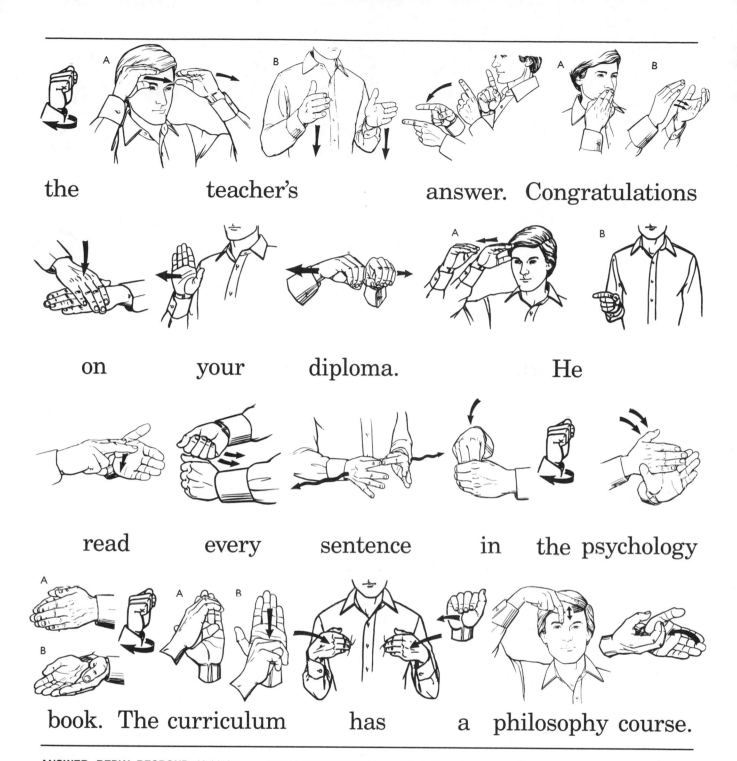

the　　　teacher's　　　answer.　Congratulations

on　　　your　　　diploma.　　　He

read　　　every　　　sentence　　　in　　the psychology

book.　The curriculum　　　has　　　a　philosophy course.

**ANSWER, REPLY, RESPOND:** Hold the right vertical index finger to the lips and place the left vertical index finger a short distance in front. Pivot both hands forward and down from the wrists so that the index fingers point forward.

**BOOK, TEXTBOOK, VOLUME:** Place the hands palm to palm, with fingers pointing forward. Open both hands to the palm-up position while maintaining contact with the little fingers.

**CONGRATULATE:** Touch the lips with the fingers of the right flat hand and then clap the hands as much as desired.

**COURSE:** Move the little-finger edge of the right *C* hand in a small arc from the left-hand fingertips to the base of the left hand.

**CURRICULUM:** Hold the thumb and index-finger side of the right hand against the fingers of the left flat hand. Move the right *C* hand down to the base of the left hand while forming an *M* hand.

**DIPLOMA:** Place the thumb and index-finger sides of both *O* hands together, then move them horizontally away from each other to the sides.

**PHILOSOPHY:** Move the right *P* hand up and down just in front of the forehead. Make the movement from the wrist.

**PSYCHOLOGY:** Place the little-finger edge of the right flat hand on the palm-forward left hand between the thumb and index fin-ger. The movement is often repeated.

**READ:** Point the right *V* fingers at the left flat palm and move them downward.

**SENTENCE:** Touch the thumb and index finger of each *F* hand in front of the chest. Pull the hands apart to the sides, with either a straight or a wavy motion.

**TEACH, EDUCATE, INDOCTRINATE, IN-STRUCT:** Position both open *and* hands at the front and sides of the head, then move them forward while simultaneously forming closed *and* hands.

LOOK IN INDEX FOR LOCATION OF ADDITIONAL DESCRIPTIONS.

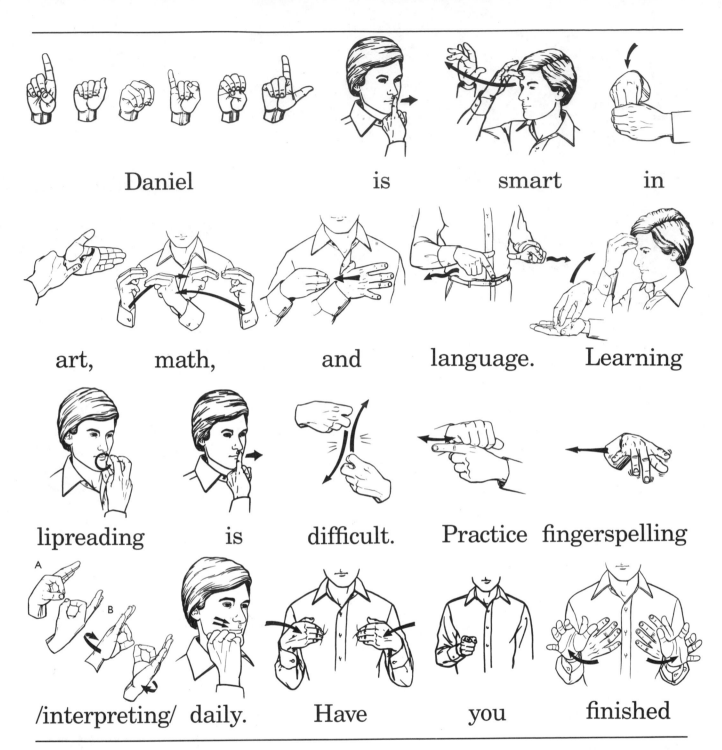

Daniel is smart in

art, math, and language. Learning

lipreading is difficult. Practice fingerspelling

/interpreting/ daily. Have you finished

**ART, DESIGN, DRAW:** Trace a wavy line over the left flat palm with the right *I* finger.

**DAILY, EVERY DAY:** Place the right *A* hand on the right cheek with the palm facing the cheek. Rub it forward several times.

**DIFFICULT, HARD:** Strike the knuckles of both bent *V* hands as they are moved up and down.

**FINGERSPELLING, ALPHABET, DACTYLOLOGY, MANUAL ALPHABET, SPELL:** With palm facing down, wiggle the fingers of the right flat open hand as the hand moves along a horizontal line to the right.

**FINISH, ALREADY:** Hold both open hands to the front with palms facing self and fin-

gers pointing up. Shake them quickly outward to the sides a few times.

**INTERPRET, TRANSLATE:** Hold the *F* hands with palms facing and left palm facing forward; then reverse hand positions.

**LANGUAGE, TONGUE:** Point both *L* hands toward each other (sometimes the index fingers point up), and move them to the sides with a twisting motion from the wrists.

**LEARN, STUDENT:** Place the fingers of the right open hand on the left upturned palm. Close the right fingers as the hand is moved to forehead. Then place fingertips on forehead. To sign *student,* add the sign

for *person* (personalizing word ending).

**LIPREADING, ORAL, SPEECHREADING:** Hold the right curved *V* fingers at the mouth. Move around the mouth in a counterclockwise direction.

**MATHEMATICS, ALGEBRA, CALCULUS, GEOMETRY, STATISTICS, TRIGONOMETRY:** Make an upward and inward motion with both *M* hands so that right *M* hand crosses inside left. Use *A* hands for *algebra, C* hands for *calculus,* and so on.

**SMART, BRIGHT, BRILLIANT, CLEVER, INTELLIGENT:** Touch the forehead with the right middle finger; then swing the right hand forward and upward.

LOOK IN INDEX FOR LOCATION OF ADDITIONAL DESCRIPTIONS.

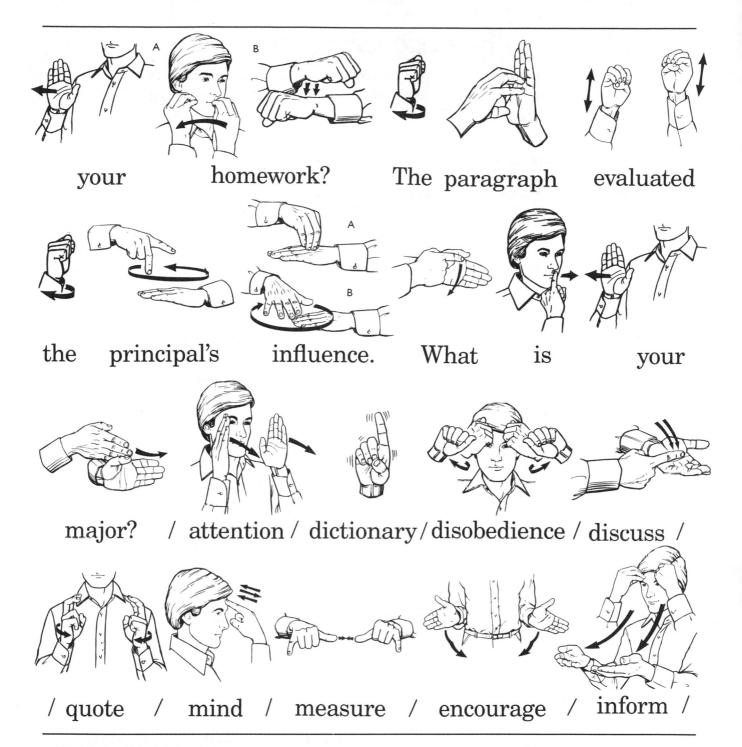

your     homework?     The   paragraph     evaluated

the     principal's     influence.     What     is     your

major?  / attention / dictionary / disobedience / discuss /

/ quote  /   mind  /   measure  /   encourage  /   inform  /

---

**DICTIONARY:** Hold the right *D* hand up and shake it.

**DISCUSS:** Strike the left palm with the right index finger several times.

**DISOBEDIENCE, DISOBEY:** Hold one or both *A* hands close to the forehead with palms facing in. Twist both hands so that palms face forward.

**EVALUATE, CONSIDER:** Move both *E* hands up and down alternately with palms facing forward.

**HOMEWORK:** Combine the signs for *home* and *work*.

**INFLUENCE:** Hold the left flat or curved hand with palm down and fingers facing right. Place the fingers of the right *and* hand

on the back of the left hand and move the right hand forward and to the right while opening the fingers.

**INFORM, INFORMATION, NOTIFY:** Place the fingers of both *and* hands on each side of the forehead, then move them in a downward forward arc to an open hand position with palms facing up.

**MAJOR, AREA, FIELD, PROFESSION, SPECIALTY:** Point the fingers of the left hand forward with palm facing right. Move the little-finger edge of the right flat hand forward along the left index finger. The right *P*-hand shape can be used to sign *profession*.

**MEASURE:** Touch the thumb tips of both *Y* hands together a few times.

**MIND, INTELLECT, MENTAL:** Tap the right index finger on the forehead a few times.

**PARAGRAPH:** Place thumb and fingertips of the right *C* hand against left flat palm.

**PRINCIPAL:** Circle the right palm-down *P* hand in a counterclockwise direction over the back of the left flat hand.

**QUOTE, CAPTION, CITE, SUBJECT, THEME, TITLE, TOPIC:** Hold both curved *V* hands to the front with palms facing forward. Twist them simultaneously so that the palms face each other.

LOOK IN INDEX FOR LOCATION OF ADDITIONAL DESCRIPTIONS.

# Practice Giving Signs

Practice signing the following sentences once again. Try to do so without referring back to the illustrations. You can also cover the page opposite if you wish.

Write your school paper.

Study your lessons and you won't fail the exam.

When do you graduate from Gallaudet College for the deaf?

Wisdom is the skillful use of knowledge.

Education can change a traditional / narrow-minded / ignorant / person into a broad-minded thinker.

The science class has sophomores.

The history / poetry / class has juniors and seniors.

The young freshman understood / misunderstood / the teacher's answer.

Congratulations on your diploma.

He read every sentence in the psychology book.

The curriculum has a philosophy course.

Daniel is smart in art, math, and language.

Learning lipreading is difficult.

Practice fingerspelling / interpreting / daily.

Have you finished your homework?

The paragraph evaluated the principal's influence.

What is your major?

/attention/dictionary/disobedience/discuss /quote/mind/measure/encourage/inform/

# Fingerspelling Practice

Practice the following words at least twice with a speed that is both steady and comfortable for you.

| | | | | | |
|---|---|---|---|---|---|
| zoologist | doctor | writer | politician | manager | mortician |
| artist | nurse | veteran | businessman | messenger | lobbyist |
| carpenter | soldier | salesman | lawyer | psychologist | journalist |
| electrician | student | fisherman | editor | judge | reporter |
| plumber | teacher | technician | reader | gardener | illustrator |
| scientist | mechanic | builder | pilot | farmer | humorist |
| radiologist | printer | captain | stewardess | dairyman | governor |

# Practice Receiving Signs

Interpret the following signs. Practicing by this method will help you receive and understand the signs more easily. Say the words out loud as you proceed.

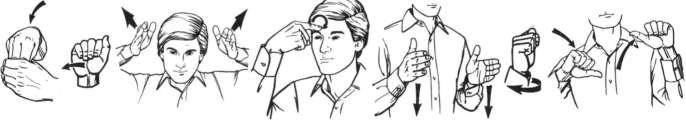

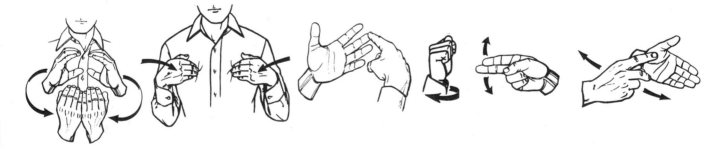

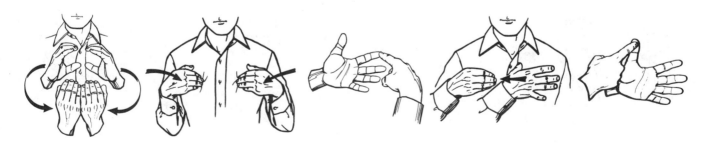

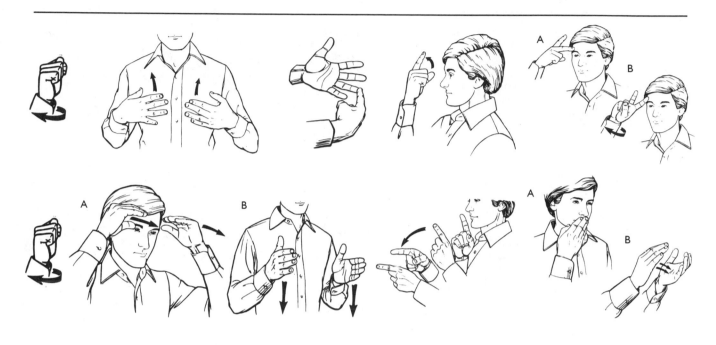

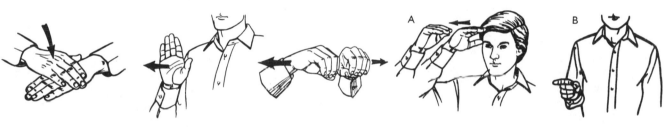

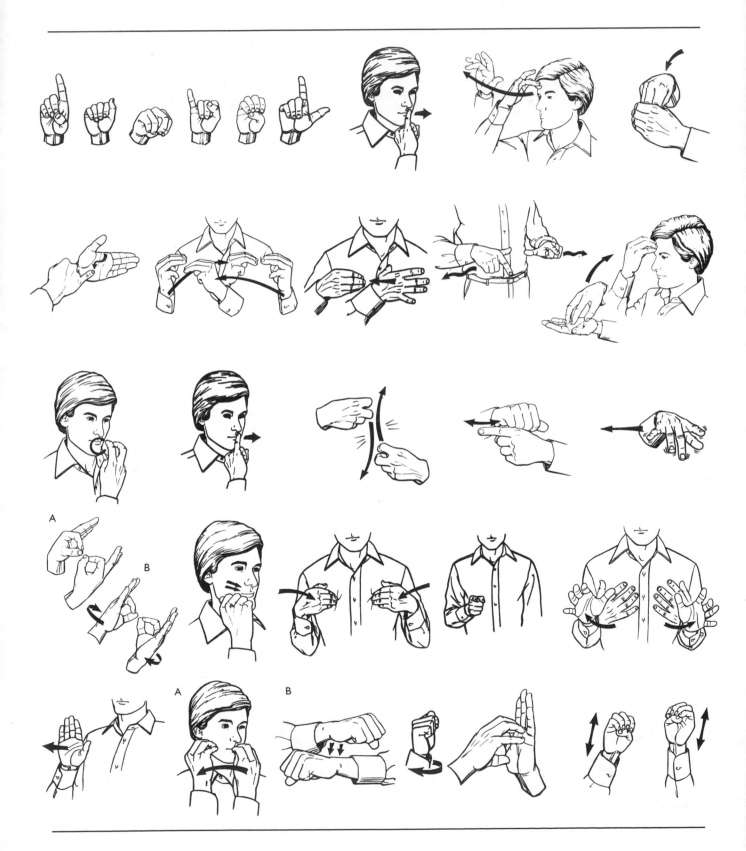

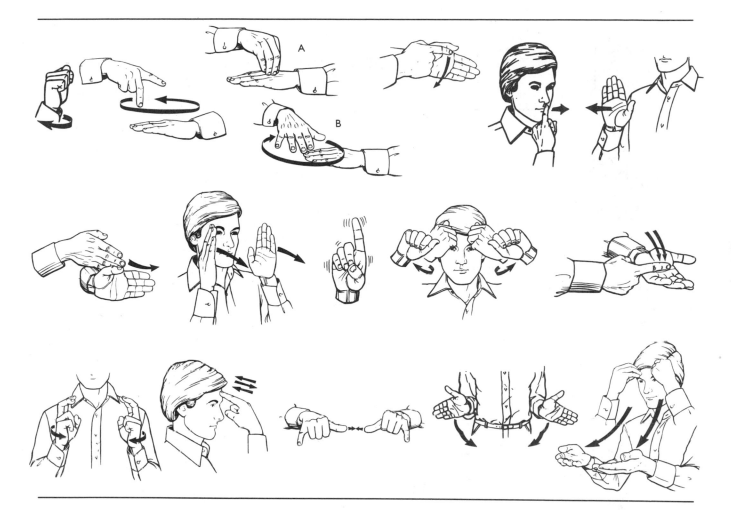

# Vocabulary Review

Identify the following signs from this and previous chapters to reinforce your vocabulary.

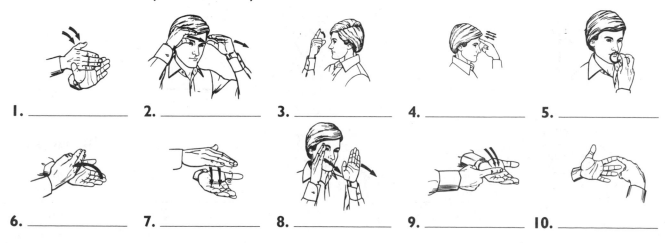

1. _____   2. _____   3. _____   4. _____   5. _____

6. _____   7. _____   8. _____   9. _____   10. _____

# Test Your Skill: Matching

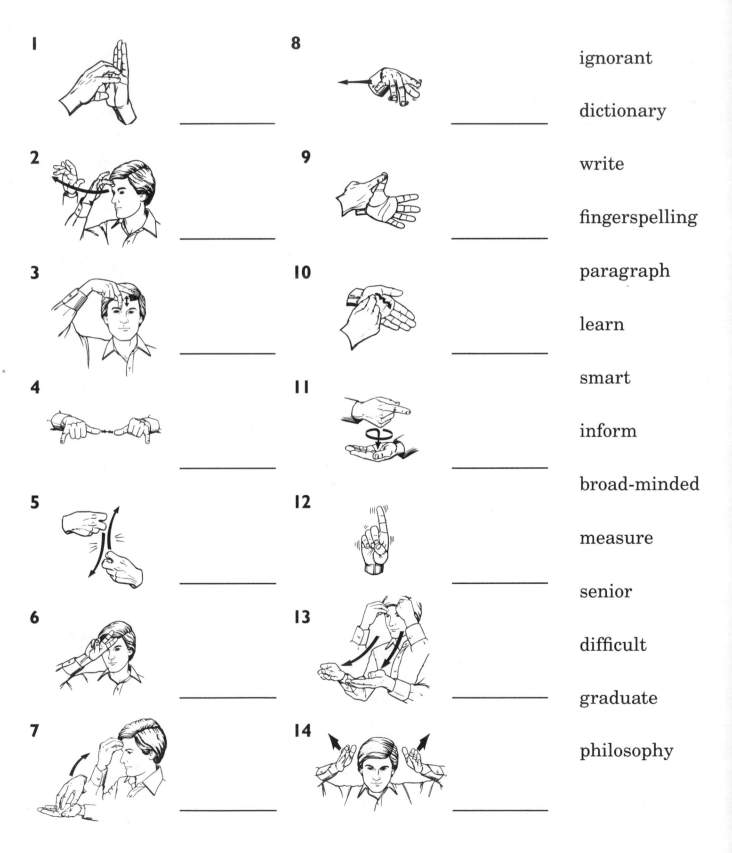

1 _____

2 _____

3 _____

4 _____

5 _____

6 _____

7 _____

8 _____

9 _____

10 _____

11 _____

12 _____

13 _____

14 _____

ignorant

dictionary

write

fingerspelling

paragraph

learn

smart

inform

broad-minded

measure

senior

difficult

graduate

philosophy

# Multiple Choice

Draw a circle around or place a check mark beside the sign that matches the italicized word. For additional practice you can sign all the words in the sentences.

1 *Practice* lipreading daily.

   A        B        C

2 Your school *paper* needs to be written soon.

   A        B        C

3 Will you *fingerspell* slowly for us?

   A        B        C

4 Be *wise* and study your lessons.

   A        B        C

5 The student failed the science *examination*.

   A        B        C

6 The young *freshman* liked his new teacher.

   A        B        C

7 Geoffrey, a sophomore, was *clever* in language study.

   A        B        C

8 How far is your *college* from here?

   A        B        C

**9** Which *paragraph* do you want me to read?

A    B    C

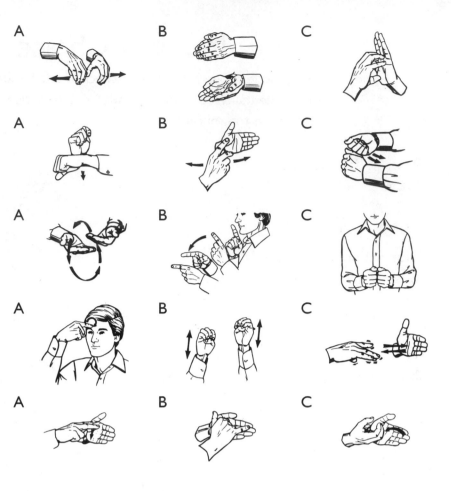

**10** She chose the *traditional* way of doing things.

A    B    C

**11** What is the *answer* to that difficult science question?

A    B    C

**12** *Evaluate* the first sentence in the book.

A    B    C

**13** What *courses* are you studying at Gallaudet?

A    B    C

# Extra Practice

Sign the following sentences which contain words chosen mainly from this chapter. This will give you additional practice using the signs you have just learned.

**1** Please interpret our principal's talk for me.

**2** Study the math book and you will pass the examination.

**3** You should know what your major is after two years in college.

**4** The teacher found it difficult to get the student's attention.

**5** Many adults need to be encouraged to get more education.

**6** Chris practiced his fingerspelling daily.

**7** My poetry class has mostly juniors and seniors.

**8** Are you broad-minded enough to change your thinking?

**9** When will you graduate?

**10** Where is the psychology class?

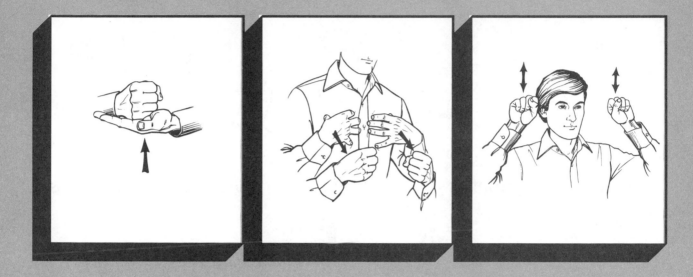

# Health
# and
# Emergencies

---

# 10

# Practice Learning Signs

Learn and practice the signs and sentences on each page before proceeding to the next. Descriptions are supplied at the bottom of each page.

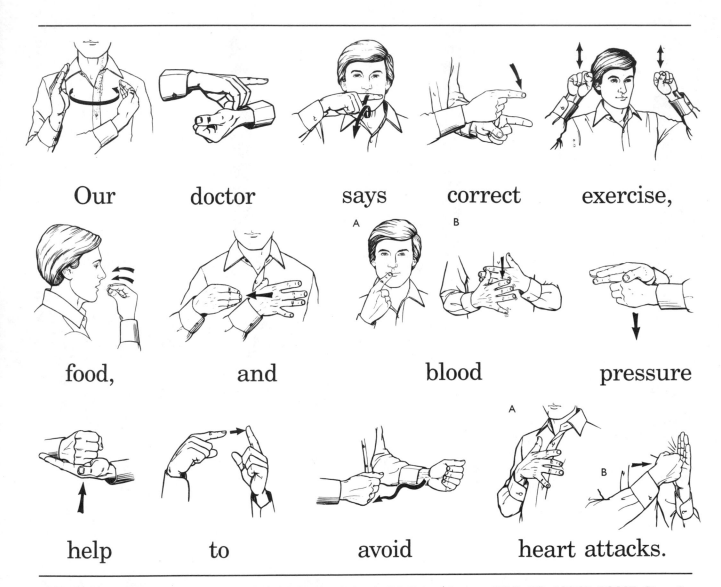

| Our | doctor | says | correct | exercise, |
|---|---|---|---|---|

| food, | and | blood | pressure |
|---|---|---|---|

| help | to | avoid | heart attacks. |
|---|---|---|---|

**AVOID, EVADE, SHUN:** Place both *A* hands to the front with palms facing and the right hand slightly behind the left. Move the right hand backward away from the left with a wavy motion. *Alternative:* Push to left with the palms of both flat hands while making an appropriate facial expression.

**BLOOD, BLEED, HEMORRHAGE:** Wiggle the fingers of the right open hand as they move down the back of the left open hand. Sometimes the lips are touched first with the right index finger, which is the sign for *red.*

**CORRECT, ACCURATE, APPROPRIATE, RIGHT, SUITABLE:** Point both index fin-gers forward and bring the little-finger edge of the right hand down onto the thumb edge of the left hand.

**DOCTOR, PHYSICIAN, PSYCHIATRY, SURGEON:** Place the right *D* hand or *M* fingers on the upturned left wrist. Use the right *P* hand for *psychiatry.*

**EXERCISE (PHYSICAL):** Hold both *S* hands up to the front with palms facing forward. Move both hands up and down (or forward and backward) simultaneously.

**HEART ATTACK:** Place the right middle finger over the heart with the other fingers extended. Close the right hand and strike the left palm sharply.

**HELP, AID, ASSIST, BOOST:** Place the right closed hand on the flat left palm and lift both hands together.

**PRESSURE:** Point the left *G* hand forward; then push down with the right flat hand on the index side of the left *G* hand.

**SAY, MENTION, REMARK, SPEAK, SPEECH, STATE, TELL:** Make a small forward circular movement in front of the mouth with the right index finger.

LOOK IN INDEX FOR LOCATION OF ADDITIONAL DESCRIPTIONS.

**168**

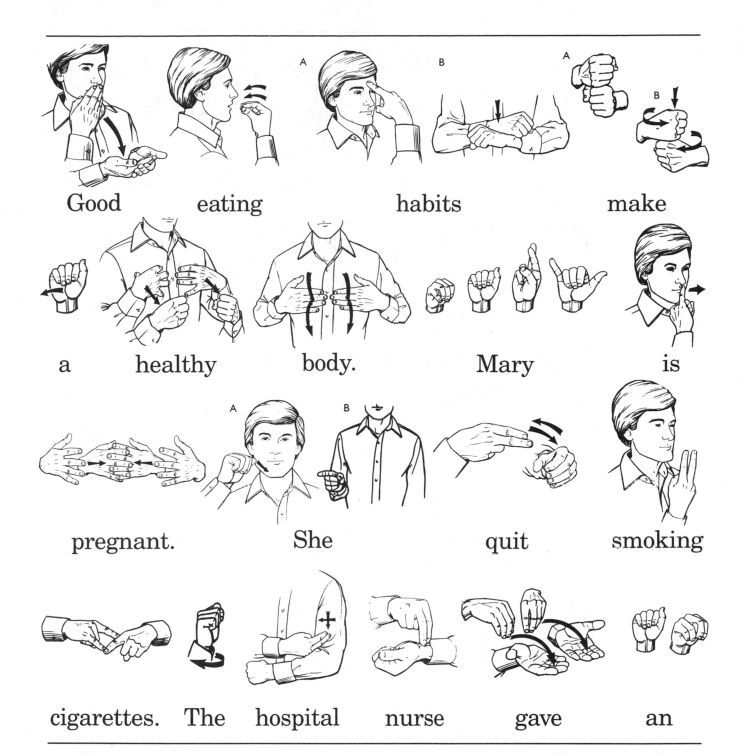

Good eating habits make

a healthy body. Mary is

pregnant. She quit smoking

cigarettes. The hospital nurse gave an

**BODY, PHYSICAL:** Place the palms of both flat hands against the chest and repeat a little lower. Sometimes one hand is used.

**CIGARETTE:** Point the left index finger in a forward direction. Extend the right index and little finger with other fingers closed. Place the right index finger on the left index knuckle and the right little finger on the left index tip.

**GIVE, DISTRIBUTE:** Hold both *and* hands to the front with palms facing down. Move them forward simultaneously while forming flat hands with fingers pointing forward and palms facing up.

**HABIT, CUSTOM, PRACTICE:** Touch the forehead with the right index finger. Change the right hand to an *S* hand as it is brought down and crosses the left *S* hand at the wrist. Push both hands down slightly.

**HEALTHY, ROBUST, WELL, WHOLE-SOME:** Place the fingertips and thumbs of both curved open hands on the chest, then move them forward while forming *S* hands.

**HOSPITAL, PATIENT:** Use the right *H* or *P* fingers for *hospital* and *patient,* respectively, and draw a cross on the upper left arm.

**NURSE:** Place the right extended *N* fingertips on the upturned left wrist.

**PREGNANT:** Interlock the fingers of both hands in front of the abdomen.

**QUIT, RESIGN:** Position the right *H* fingers in the left *C* hand and pull them out sharply.

**SMOKING:** Hold the right *V* fingers in front of the lips with palm facing in.

LOOK IN INDEX FOR LOCATION OF ADDITIONAL DESCRIPTIONS.

injection   to   fight   pneumonia. The medicine

and   pills   stopped   his   pain.

Jill   was   nervous / frightened / after

the   accident / earthquake /. The   X ray

**ACCIDENT, COLLISION, CRASH, HIT, WRECK:** Strike the knuckles of both clenched hands together. *Hit* can be signed by striking the knuckles of the right closed hand against the left upright index finger.
**EARTHQUAKE:** Grasp the back of the left closed hand between the right index finger and thumb; then pivot the right hand back and forth (toward the left fingers and elbow). Move both fists forward and backward in front of the body with forceful movements. *Note:* These movements combine the signs for *earth* and *thunder.*
**FIGHTING, BOXING:** Place the right *S* hand close to the body and the left *S* hand a short distance from the body. Reverse posi-

tions a few times.
**FRIGHTENED, AFRAID, SCARED, TERRIFIED:** Move both *and* hands simultaneously across the chest from the sides in opposite directions. During the movement, change the hand positions to open hands.
**INJECTION, SHOT, SYRINGE:** Place the curved thumb and the index and middle fingers of the right hand at the upper left arm and move the thumb toward the curved fingers.
**MEDICINE, DRUG, PRESCRIPTION:** Make small circles on the left palm with the right middle finger.
**PAIN, ACHE, HURT, INJURY, WOUND:** Thrust the index fingers toward each other

several times. This may be done adjacent to the particular area of the body that is suffering from pain.
**PILL, CAPSULE, TAKE A PILL:** Imitate putting a pill into the mouth with the right thumb and index finger.
**PNEUMONIA:** Place the middle fingers of both *P* hands against the chest. Rock them up and down while maintaining contact with the chest.
**STOP, CEASE, HALT:** Bring the little-finger side of the right flat hand down sharply at right angles on the left palm.
**X RAY:** Sign *X;* then form the *O* hand with palm facing self. Open the *O* hand as it is moved toward the chest.

LOOK IN INDEX FOR LOCATION OF ADDITIONAL DESCRIPTIONS.

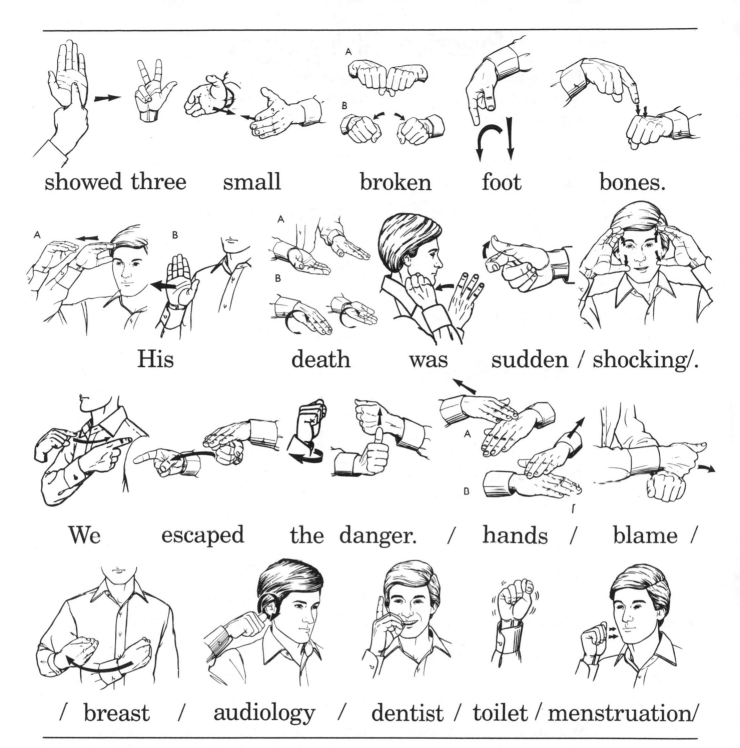

showed three small broken foot bones.

His death was sudden / shocking/.

We escaped the danger. / hands / blame /

/ breast / audiology / dentist / toilet / menstruation/

**BLAME, ACCUSE, FAULT, MY FAULT, YOUR FAULT:** Strike the back of the closed left hand with the little-finger edge of the right A hand. Point the right knuckles and thumb to self or another, depending on who is being referred to. Combine the movements together smoothly as one.

**BONES:** Close the left downturned hand and tap the knuckles with the right X finger.

**DANGER, PERIL:** Move the back of the right A thumb up across the back of the left hand a few times.

**DEATH, DEAD, DIE, EXPIRE, PERISH:** Hold both flat hands to the front with the right palm facing up and the left palm facing down. Move both hands in an arc to the left while changing the hand positions so that the palms reverse direction.

**DENTIST:** Touch the teeth with the thumb of the right D hand.

**ESCAPE, FLEE, RUN OFF:** Point the right index finger forward and place it under the left flat palm. Move the right index finger quickly forward and to the right.

**FEET:** Point to one foot, then the other.

**HANDS:** Place the right downturned hand over the back of the left downturned hand. Move the right hand toward self, and repeat the action with the left hand over the right.

**SHOCK, BEWILDER, DUMBFOUND, STUN:** Circle the eyes with both C hands

and suddenly open the hands to a wide C position.

**SHOW, DEMONSTRATE, EXAMPLE:** Place the right index finger in the left palm, and move both hands forward.

**SMALL, LITTLE (MEASURE, SIZE):** Hold both flat hands to the front with palms facing; then move them closer to each other in short stages.

**SUDDENLY, FAST, IMMEDIATELY, QUICK, RAPID, SPEEDY, SWIFT:** Flick the right thumb from the crooked index finger.

LOOK IN INDEX FOR LOCATION OF ADDITIONAL DESCRIPTIONS.

# Practice Giving Signs

Practice signing the following sentences once again. Try to do so without referring back to the illustrations. You can also cover the page opposite if you wish.

Our doctor says correct exercise, food, and blood pressure help to avoid heart attacks.

Good eating habits make a healthy body.

Mary is pregnant.

She quit smoking cigarettes.

The hospital nurse gave an injection to fight pneumonia.

The medicine and pills stopped his pain.

Jill was nervous /frightened/ after the accident /earthquake/.

The X ray showed three small broken foot bones.

His death was sudden /shocking/.

We escaped the danger.

/hands/blame/breast/audiology/dentist/toilet/ menstruation/

# Fingerspelling Practice

Practice the following words at least twice with a speed that is both steady and comfortable for you.

| | | | | | |
|---|---|---|---|---|---|
| Reagan | Johnson | Grant | Tyler | Fillmore | Wilson |
| Carter | Hoover | Polk | Harrison | Garfield | Churchill |
| Ford | Roosevelt | Cleveland | Jefferson | Taylor | Thatcher |
| Nixon | Coolidge | Madison | Adams | Hayes | Constitution |
| Kennedy | Harding | Van Buren | Buchanan | Monroe | Congress |
| Eisenhower | Taft | Jackson | Pierce | Washington | Caesar |
| Truman | Wilson | McKinley | Arthur | Lincoln | Alexander |

# Practice Receiving Signs

Interpret the following signs. Practicing by this method will help you receive and understand the signs more easily. Say the words out loud as you proceed.

The    flood    was    destructive,    but

not    one    person    was    killed.    Some

children    get    mumps    and    measles.

The    operation    on    my    arm /   eye /

**ARM:** Move the fingertips of the right up-turned curved hand down the left arm.

**CHILD, CHILDREN:** Place the right flat downturned hand before the body and motion as if patting the head of a child. When referring to more than one child, move the hand to another position and repeat the sign.

**DESTROY, ABOLISH, DAMAGE, DEMOL-ISH:** Put both open hands to the front with palms facing and the right hand lower than the left. Reverse the hand positions while forming A hands; then reverse them again to the original position while still maintaining A hands.

**EYE:** Point to the eye with the right index finger.

**FLOOD:** Touch the mouth with the index finger of the right W hand a few times (the sign for *water*). Point both palm-down open hands forward and raise them simultaneously while wiggling the fingers.

**KILL, MURDER, SLAY:** Place the left slightly curved hand to the front with palm facing down. Move the right index finger under the left hand while simultaneously giving it a clockwise twist.

**MEASLES:** Tap the right side of the face in several places with the fingertips of the right curved open hand.

**MUMPS:** Place the curved fingertips of both hands at the neck and move outward slightly.

**OPERATION, INCISION, SURGERY:** Move the right A thumbnail down (or across) the chest or abdomen.

**SOME, PART, PORTION, SECTION:** Place the little-finger edge of the right slightly curved hand onto the left flat palm. Pull the right hand toward self while forming a flat right hand.

LOOK IN INDEX FOR LOCATION OF ADDITIONAL DESCRIPTIONS.

was    successful.    Yesterday    his

sickness    made    him    suffer    with

coughing    and    dizziness.    The    poison    made

him    vomit    /    weak    /.    I

**COUGH:** Strike the chest sharply a few times with the fingertips of the right curved open hand. The signer may also open the mouth and simulate a coughing action while signing.

**DIZZY:** Hold the palm side of the right curved open hand in front of the face and move it in a few slow counterclockwise circles.

**POISON:** Make small circles on the left palm with the middle finger of the right *P* hand.

**SICK, DISEASE, ILL:** Place the right middle finger on the forehead and the left middle finger on the stomach. Assume an appropriate facial expression.

**SUCCESS, ACCOMPLISH, PROSPER, SUCCEED:** Point both index fingers toward each other or toward the head; then move them upward while simultaneously making little forward circles. End with both index fingers pointing up and palms facing forward.

**SUFFER, AGONY, ENDURE:** Slowly revolve right *S* hand in a forward circle around left stationary *S* hand. Assume appropriate facial expression.

**VOMIT, THROW UP:** Move both open hands forward and down from the mouth. Sometimes one hand is used and the mouth is opened while the head tilts forward.

**WEAK, FEEBLE, FRAIL:** Place the right curved fingers in a standing position in the palm of the left flat hand. Cause the fingers to bend and unbend.

**YESTERDAY:** With the palm facing forward, place the thumb of the right *A* (or *Y*) hand on the right side of the chin. Move in a backward arc toward the ear.

LOOK IN INDEX FOR LOCATION OF ADDITIONAL DESCRIPTIONS.

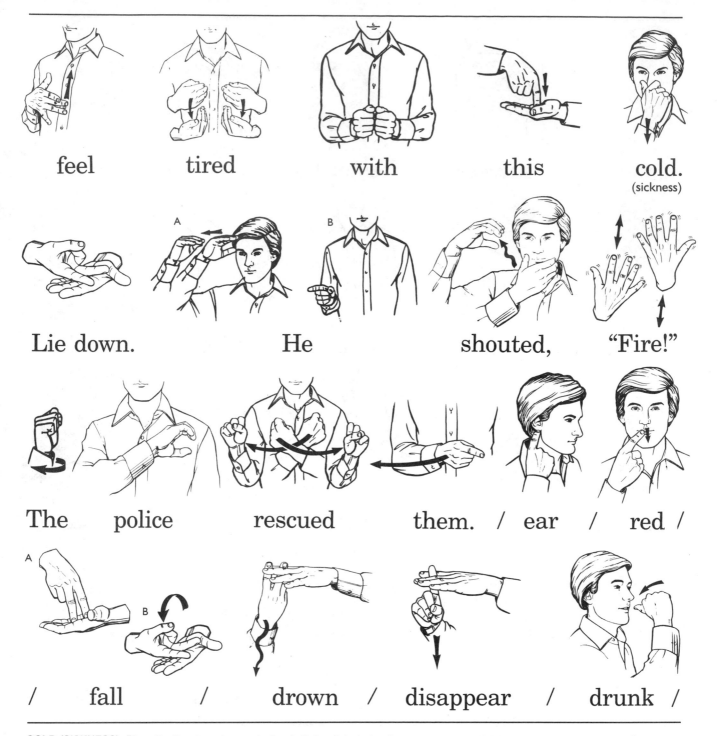

feel          tired          with          this          cold.
(sickness)

Lie down.          He          shouted,          "Fire!"

The          police          rescued          them.  /  ear  /  red /

/  fall  /          drown  /  disappear  /  drunk  /

**COLD (SICKNESS):** Place the thumb and bent index finger on either side of the nose and draw down a few times.

**DISAPPEAR:** Move the right index finger downward between the index and middle fingers of the left palm-down flat hand.

**DROWN:** Move the right V fingers down from between the left index and middle fingers with a slight wavy movement.

**FALL:** Stand the right V fingers in the left flat palm. Flip them over so that the back of the V fingers rests on the left palm.

**FIRE, BURN, FLAME, HELL:** With palms facing in, move both slightly curved open hands up and down alternately in front of the body while wiggling the fingers. When

signing *hell*, the right index finger can be pointed down as an addition.

**LIE DOWN, RECLINE:** Place the back of the right V fingers on the left flat palm.

**POLICE, COP, SHERIFF:** Place the thumb side of the right C hand at the left shoulder.

**RESCUE, DELIVER, FREE, INDEPENDENT, LIBERTY, REDEEM, SAFE, SALVATION, SAVIOR:** Cross the closed hands on the chest with palms facing in; then rotate them to the sides with palms facing forward. Most signers prefer to initialize each word. For example: Use an R for *rescue;* a D for *deliver;* etc. The observer's understanding is aided by the context.

**SHOUT, CALL OUT, CRY OUT, ROAR,**

**SCREAM:** Place either the right C or curved open hand in front of the mouth and move it forward and upward with a wavy motion.

**THIS:** Put the right index fingertip into the palm of the left upturned flat palm.

**TIRED, EXHAUSTED, FATIGUED, WEARY:** Place the fingertips of both bent hands on the upper chest, then pivot the hands downward while maintaining contact with the chest. The fingertips point upward in the final position.

LOOK IN INDEX FOR LOCATION OF ADDITIONAL DESCRIPTIONS.

# Practice Giving Signs

Practice signing the following sentences once again. Try to do so without referring back to the illustrations. You can also cover the page opposite if you wish.

The flood was destructive but not one person was killed.

Some children get mumps and measles.

The operation on my arm /eye/ was successful.

Yesterday his sickness made him suffer with coughing and dizziness.

The poison made him vomit /weak/.

I feel tired with this cold.

Lie down.

He shouted, "Fire!"

The police rescued them.

/ear/red/fall/drown/disappear/drunk/

# Vocabulary Review

Identify the following signs from this and previous chapters to reinforce your vocabulary.

1. _____   2. _____   3. _____   4. _____   5. _____

6. _____   7. _____   8. _____   9. _____   10. _____

11. _____   12. _____   13. _____   14. _____   15. _____

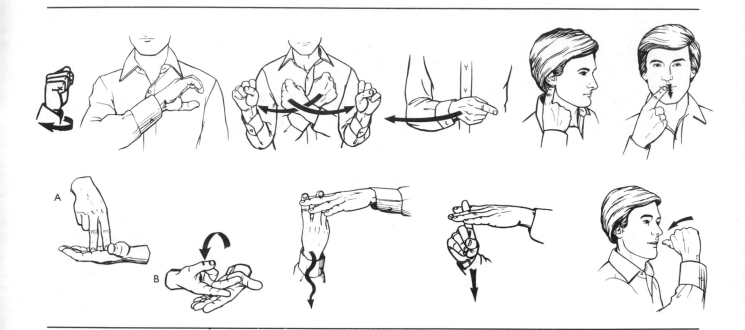

# Test Your Skill: Matching

This section uses standard matching techniques. See if you can match the signs with the words by writing the correct word next to the sign.

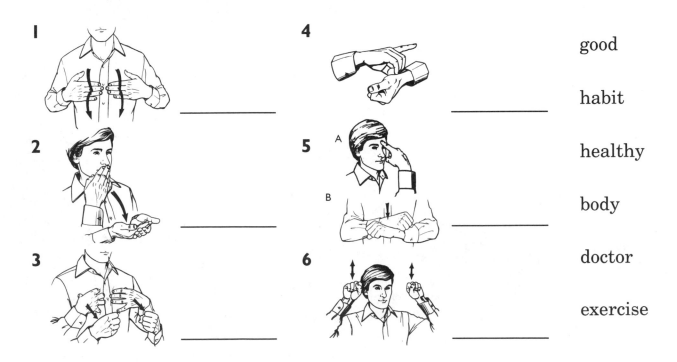

good

habit

healthy

body

doctor

exercise

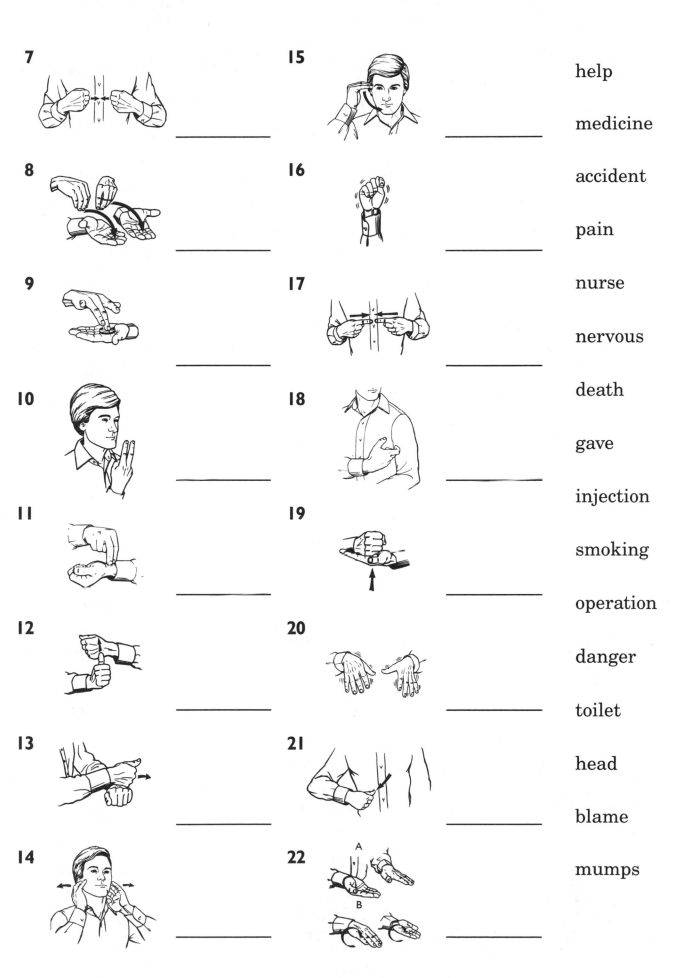

7 _____

8 _____

9 _____

10 _____

11 _____

12 _____

13 _____

14 _____

15 _____

16 _____

17 _____

18 _____

19 _____

20 _____

21 _____

22 _____

help

medicine

accident

pain

nurse

nervous

death

gave

injection

smoking

operation

danger

toilet

head

blame

mumps

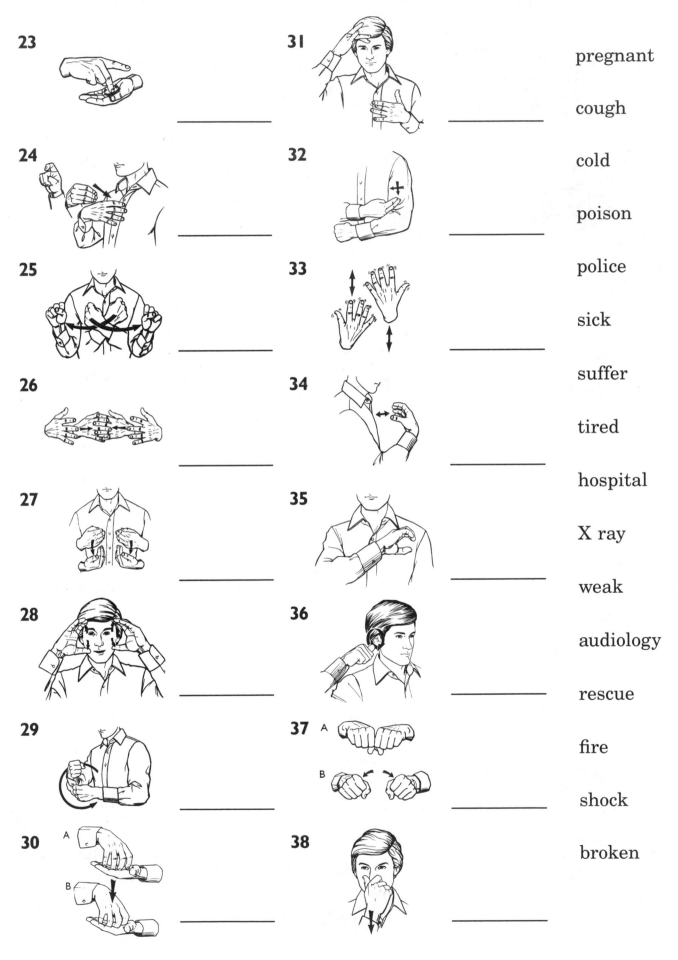

**23** _____

**24** _____

**25** _____

**26** _____

**27** _____

**28** _____

**29** _____

**30** A  B _____

**31** _____

**32** _____

**33** _____

**34** _____

**35** _____

**36** _____

**37** A  B _____

**38** _____

pregnant

cough

cold

poison

police

sick

suffer

tired

hospital

X ray

weak

audiology

rescue

fire

shock

broken

# Multiple Choice

Draw a circle around or place a check mark beside the sign that matches the italicized word. For additional practice you can sign all the words in the sentences.

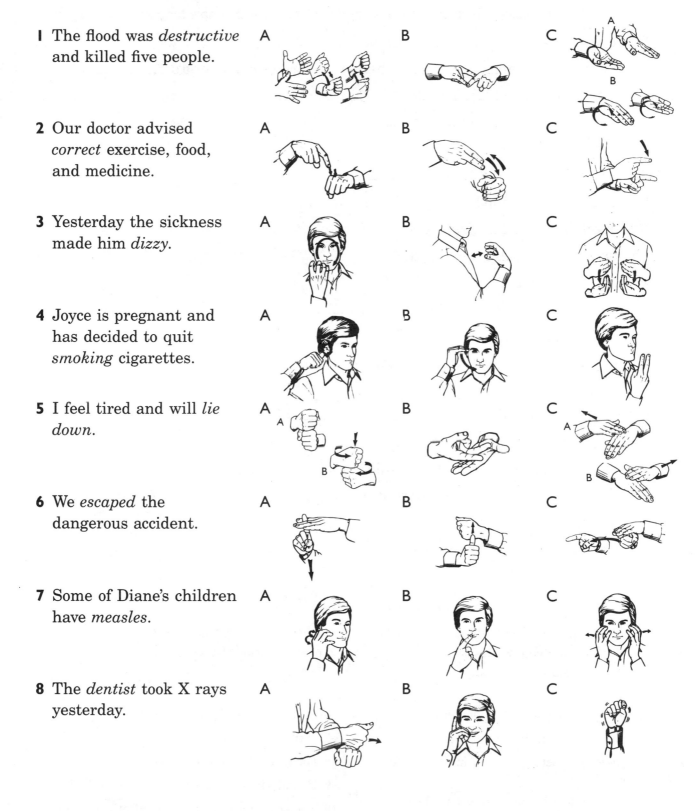

**1** The flood was *destructive* and killed five people.    A    B    C

**2** Our doctor advised *correct* exercise, food, and medicine.    A    B    C

**3** Yesterday the sickness made him *dizzy*.    A    B    C

**4** Joyce is pregnant and has decided to quit *smoking* cigarettes.    A    B    C

**5** I feel tired and will *lie down*.    A    B    C

**6** We *escaped* the dangerous accident.    A    B    C

**7** Some of Diane's children have *measles*.    A    B    C

**8** The *dentist* took X rays yesterday.    A    B    C

# Fill In the Blanks

Sign the following sentences and choose an appropriate sign for the blank spaces. Use the skill you have gained thus far to complete the sentences logically. There may be more than one answer for each blank space. The first one is already completed as an example for you.

1. The poison made him <u>weak</u> and <u>dizzy</u>.
2. She went into sudden _____ when she heard of her friend's _____.
3. Jill went to the _____ with a _____ foot.
4. The _____ did not stop the _____.
5. Eat good food for a _____ _____.
6. Doris is happy she quit smoking _____.
7. The _____ rescued three children from _____.
8. The sudden _____ frightened everyone.
9. No one was _____ during the _____.
10. We _____ the _____ fire.
11. My _____ is better since the _____.
12. Earl got a _____ last _____.
13. Don't _____ me for what happened.
14. Yesterday we went to the _____.
15. I am _____ and will _____ _____.
16. He has a bad _____ and _____.
17. The _____ gave some of the children an _____.
18. The _____ was put out before it did any _____.
19. Do correct _____ every day.
20. Everyone _____ the danger.

# Extra Practice

Sign the following sentences which contain words chosen mainly from this chapter. This will give you additional practice using the signs you have just learned.

1. My son took the medicine he needed.
2. What month were you in the hospital?
3. Edward said to practice good eating habits for better health.
4. Our house was lost in the destructive flood.
5. Linda went to the hospital for X rays.
6. Success comes by much work.
7. Hurry, there is a fire!
8. For a strong body, exercise.
9. Usually he does not complain when he is sick.
10. The children were nervous after the accident.

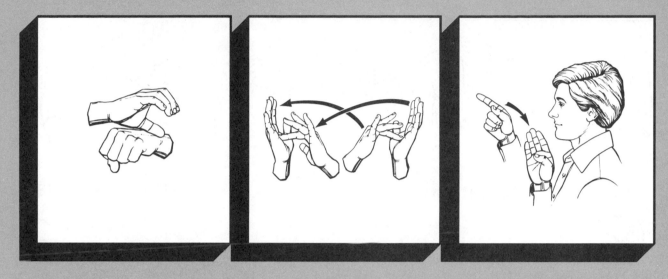

# Religion

---

## 11

---

# Practice Learning Signs

Learn and practice the signs and sentences on each page before proceeding to the next. Descriptions are supplied at the bottom of each page.

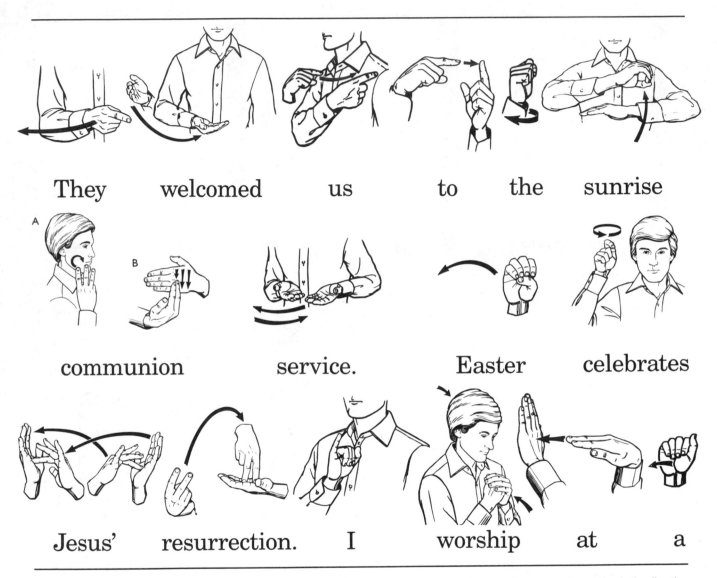

They welcomed us to the sunrise

communion service. Easter celebrates

Jesus' resurrection. I worship at a

**CELEBRATION, CHEER, HALLELUJAH, TRIUMPH, VICTORY:** Hold up one or both closed hands with the thumb tips and index fingertips touching. Make small circular movements. The *V* hands can be used for *victory.* When signing *hallelujah,* clap the hands once, then proceed with the basic sign.

**COMMUNION, EUCHARIST:** Draw the little-finger edge of the right hand downward over the back of the left flat hand which has palm facing self. Make a forward circular movement with the right *W* hand on the right cheek. This is a combination of the signs for *bread* and *wine.*

**JESUS:** Hold both open and slightly curved hands to the front with palms facing. Touch the left palm with the right middle finger; then touch the right palm with the left middle finger.

**RESURRECTION:** Hold the left flat hand to the front with palm facing up. Bring the right *V* hand up from a palm-up position until the *V* fingers stand on the left palm.

**SERVICE:** Move both upturned flat hands back and forth a few times.

**SUNRISE, SUNSET:** The left flat hand points to the right hand across the chest with palm facing down. The right *O* hand makes an upward (*sunrise*) or downward (*sunset*) arc in front of the left arm.

**THEY, THAT, THEM, THESE:** Point the right index finger forward or in the direction of the persons or objects referred to, then move it to the right.

**WELCOME:** Position the right flat hand forward and to the right with the palm facing left. Sweep the hand in toward the body until the palm is facing in front of the abdomen.

**WORSHIP, ADORE, AMEN:** Close the left hand over the right closed hand and move them slowly toward self. *Note:* A fairly common alternative for *amen* is to bring the little-finger edge of the right *A* hand down into the left flat palm.

LOOK IN INDEX FOR LOCATION OF ADDITIONAL DESCRIPTIONS.

Catholic / Episcopalian / church. The        lady

knelt        to        pray        /meditate/

at        the        altar.        Miracles        still

happen.    The    gospel    is    God's    plan

**ALTAR:** Move the *A* hands sideways in opposite directions from a central position, then down a short distance.

**CATHOLIC:** Outline a cross in front of the forehead with the right *U* fingers. Move first down, then from left to right.

**CHURCH, CHAPEL, DENOMINATION:** Place the thumb of the right *C* hand on the back of the closed left hand.

**EPISCOPAL:** Outline a priest's enlarged sleeve under the left forearm with the right index finger.

**GOD:** Point the right *G* finger in a forward-upward direction at head level. (Some signers use the whole flat hand with the palm facing left.) Move the right hand in a backward-downward arc toward self, ending with a *B* hand in front of the upper chest with palm still facing left.

**GOSPEL:** Slide the little-finger edge of the right *G* hand across the flat left hand from fingertips to heel a few times.

**HAPPEN, EVENT, OCCUR:** Point index fingers up with palms facing. Pivot hands forward from the wrists so palms face forward.

**KNEEL, PROTESTANT:** Imitate kneeling legs with the fingers of the right *V* hand on the left flat palm.

**LADY:** First sign *female;* follow with *fine.*

**MEDITATE:** Make forward circles with the right *M* hand near the right temple.

**MIRACLE, MARVEL:** Move the flat open hands up and forward a few times. Follow with the *work* sign.

**PLAN, ARRANGE, ORDER, PREPARE, READY, SYSTEM:** Place both flat hands to the front and off to the left with palms facing and fingers pointing forward. Move hands simultaneously to the right while moving them up and down slightly. *Plan* can be signed with *P* hands, *ready* with *R* hands.

**STILL, STAY:** Move the right *Y* hand in a downward-forward arc. *Stay* is usually signed with just a downward movement.

LOOK IN INDEX FOR LOCATION OF ADDITIONAL DESCRIPTIONS.

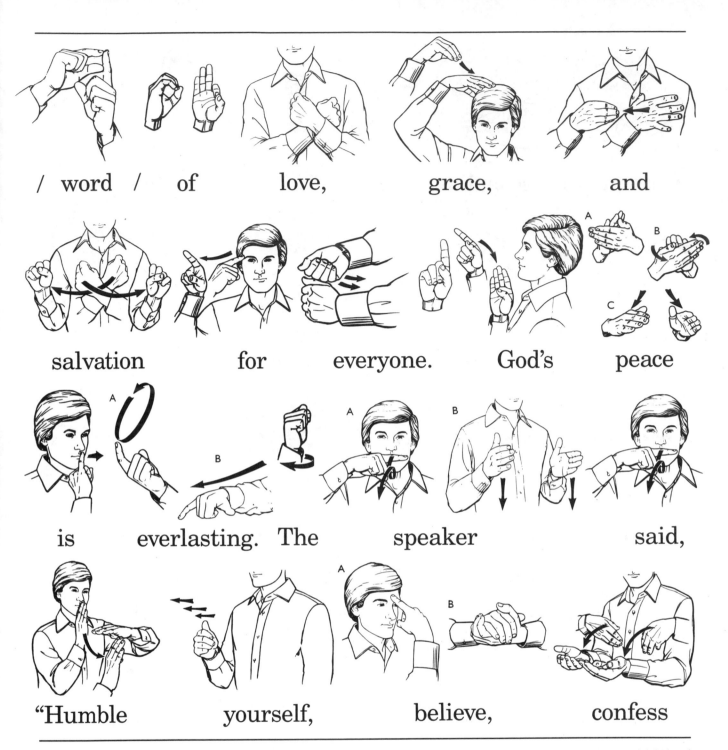

/ word / of love, grace, and

salvation for everyone. God's peace

is everlasting. The speaker said,

"Humble yourself, believe, confess

**BELIEVE:** Touch the forehead with the right index finger; then bring the right hand down to clasp the left hand in front of the chest.
**GRACE:** Move the right *and* hand down over the head while changing it to a slightly curved open hand.
**HUMBLE, MEEK, MODEST:** Point the left flat hand to the right with palm down. Touch the lips with the index finger of the right *B* hand and move it down and forward under the left hand. The head is often bowed simultaneously.
**PEACE:** Place the right flat hand on the left flat hand at chest level; then place the left on the right. Now move both flat hands down and to the sides with palms down.

Pass from one position to another smoothly and continuously.
**SALVATION, DELIVER, FREE, INDEPENDENT, LIBERTY, REDEEM, RESCUE, SAFE, SAVIOR:** Cross the closed hands on the chest with palms facing in; then rotate them to the sides with palms facing forward. Many signers prefer to initialize each word. For example, use an *R* for *rescue*, a *D* for *deliver*, etc. The receiver's understanding is aided by the context.
**SAY, MENTION, REMARK, SPEAK, SPEECH, STATE, TELL:** Make a small forward circular movement in front of the mouth with the right index finger.
**SPEAK, SPEECH, LECTURE, TESTI-**

**MONY:** Pivot the slightly curved right hand back and forth to the right of the mouth. Use a *T* hand for *testimony*.
**WORD:** Hold the left index finger up with palm facing left; then place the thumb and index finger of the right *Q* hand against it.
**YOURSELF, HERSELF, HIMSELF, ITSELF, ONESELF, THEMSELVES, YOURSELVES:** Hold the right *A*-hand thumb up and make several short forward movements in the direction of the person or object referred to.

LOOK IN INDEX FOR LOCATION OF ADDITIONAL DESCRIPTIONS.

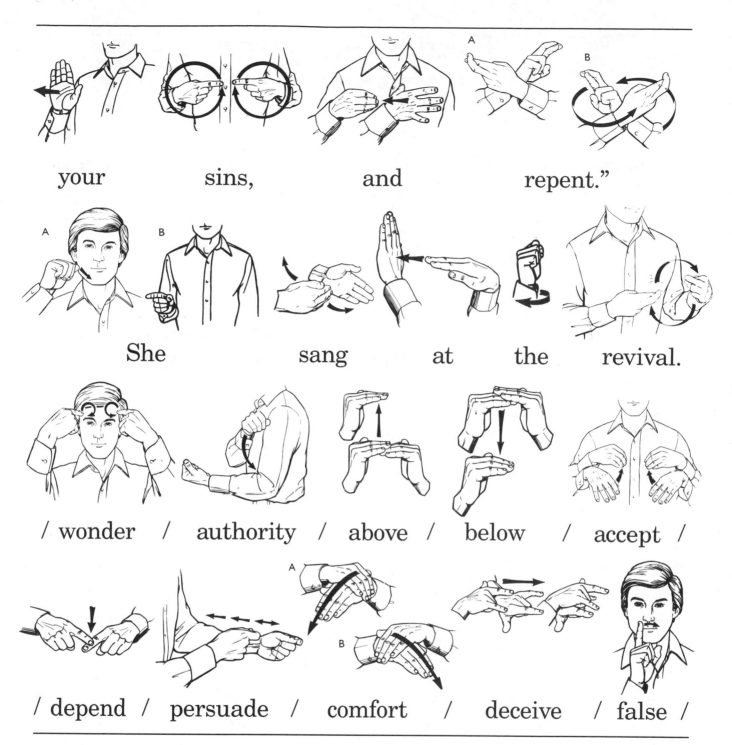

your    sins,    and    repent."

She    sang    at    the    revival.

/ wonder / authority / above / below / accept /

/ depend / persuade / comfort / deceive / false /

**ACCEPT:** Move open hands to chest while simultaneously forming *and* hands.

**AUTHORITY, ENERGY:** Make a downward arc with the right *A* hand (or curved hand) from the left shoulder to the inside of the left elbow. Use the *E* hand for *energy*.

**DECEIVE, BETRAY, FRAUD:** Point both modified *Y* hands forward with the index fingers also extended and palms down. Position one hand over the other (either is acceptable), and move the top one forward and backward a few times.

**DEPEND, RELY:** Cross the right index finger over the top of the left index finger with palms facing down, then move both hands down a short distance.

**FALSE, ARTIFICIAL, COUNTERFEIT, FAKE, PSEUDO, SHAM:** Point the right index finger up and move it across the lips from right to left.

**PERSUADE, COAX, PROD, URGE:** Move both modified *A* hands (thumb tips in crook of index fingers) back and forth while drawing them toward self.

**REPENT:** Cross the right *R* wrist over the left *R* wrist with palms facing. Reverse the position by twisting the hands at the wrist.

**REVIVAL, REVIVE:** Brush the *R* fingers alternately upward over the heart with circular motions. To sign *revive,* bring the *R* hands straight up the chest without a circular motion.

**SIN, EVIL, CRIME, WICKED:** Point both index fingers toward each other with palms facing self. Move them simultaneously in up-out-down-in circles.

**SING, HYMN, MELODY, MUSIC, SONG:** Wave the right flat hand from left to right in front of the left flat hand, which has its palm facing right. The *M* hand can be used for *music.*

**WONDER, CONCERN, CONSIDER, PONDER:** Point either both index fingers or both *W* hands toward the forehead and rotate in small circles. Sometimes only the right hand is used.

LOOK IN INDEX FOR LOCATION OF ADDITIONAL DESCRIPTIONS.

# Practice Giving Signs

Practice signing the following sentences once again. Try to do so without referring back to the illustrations. You can also cover the page opposite if you wish.

They welcomed us to the sunrise communion service.

Easter celebrates Jesus' resurrection.

I worship at a Catholic /Episcopalian/ church.

The lady knelt to pray /meditate/ at the altar.

Miracles still happen.

The gospel is God's plan /word/ of love, grace, and salvation for everyone.

God's peace is everlasting.

The speaker said, "Humble yourself, believe, confess your sins, and repent."

She sang at the revival.

/wonder/authority/above/below/accept/depend/persuade/comfort/deceive/false/

# Fingerspelling Practice

Practice the following words at least twice with a speed that is both steady and comfortable for you.

| | | | | | |
|---|---|---|---|---|---|
| Campbell | Foster | Hawkins | Matthews | Richardson | Welsh |
| White | Williams | Parks | Garrett | Ward | Lindsey |
| Isaac | Bell | Adams | O'Conners | Quin | Swanson |
| Vogel | Christianson | Anderson | Estes | Zey | Ulrich |
| Kelly | Gold | Martin | Brown | Smith | McIntosh |
| Young | Thompson | Marsh | Jones | Davidson | Higgins |
| Patterson | Parker | Rhodes | Shaffer | Wray | Howell |

# Practice Receiving Signs

Interpret the following signs. Practicing by this method will help you receive and understand the signs more easily. Say the words out loud as you proceed.

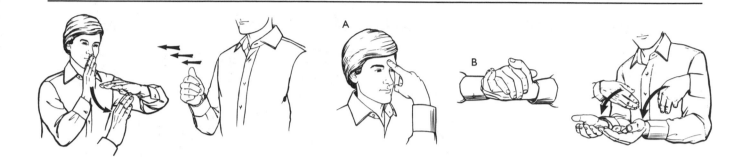

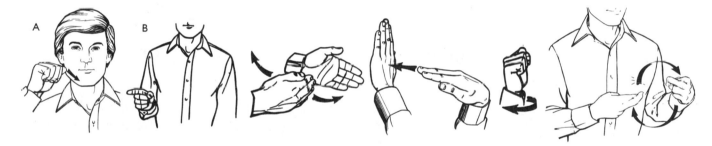

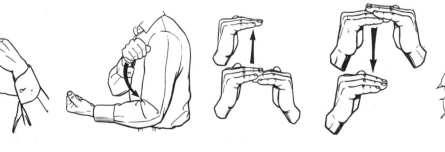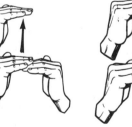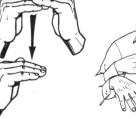

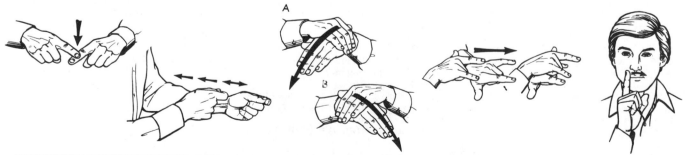

The missionary's ministry / vision / was

lost souls. The Bible says love

and forgive your neighbors. The

Lord brings truth / life /. Moses

**BIBLE, GOD'S BOOK:** Sign *Jesus* and *book. Alternative:* Point praying hands first upward, then forward, and then open them.
**BRING, FETCH:** Move both palm-up flat hands to the right or left, toward self or another, depending on who is indicated.
**FORGIVE, EXCUSE, EXEMPT, PARDON:** Stroke the lower part of the left flat hand with the right fingertips several times.
**LIFE:** Draw both open hands up the chest while wiggling the fingers. *L* hands can also be used.
**LORD, CHRIST, KING, QUEEN, ROYAL:** Move the right *L* hand from the left shoulder to the right waist. Initialize the other words with the same basic movement.

**MINISTRY:** Tap the wrist of the left down-turned closed hand with the wrist of the right downturned *M* hand a few times.
**MISSION, MISSIONARY:** Make a counterclockwise circle with the right *M* hand over the heart. To sign *missionary,* add the sign for *person* (personalizing word ending).
**MOSES:** Place the *Q* fingers of both hands at the temples with the palms facing each other. Close the fingers as the hands are moved to the sides.
**SOUL:** Place the thumb and index of the modified right *F* hand in the left *O* hand, then raise the right hand.
**TRUE, AUTHENTIC, GENUINE, REAL,**

**REALLY, SINCERE, SURE, TRUTH, VALID:** With palm facing left, move the right index finger in a forward arc from the lips.
**VISION, FORECAST, FORESEE, PROPHECY, PROPHET:** With the palm facing in, point to the eyes with the right *V* fingers. Move the right hand forward, turning the palm outward as it passes under the left flat palm. To sign *prophet,* add the sign for *person* (personalizing word ending).

LOOK IN INDEX FOR LOCATION OF ADDITIONAL DESCRIPTIONS.

sacrificed    lambs    at    Passover. The    Trinity

includes    the    Holy    Spirit.    My    congregation

faithfully    tithes.    The    devil    lies.    Our

city    has    Baptists, Assemblies of God,

**BAPTIST, BAPTISM, IMMERSION:** Move and twist both *A* hands to the right with right palm ending face up and left face down. Some do this sign in the opposite direction.
**CITY, COMMUNITY, TOWN, VILLAGE:** Make the point of a triangle with both flat hands in front of the chest. Repeat a few times while moving the hands to the right.
**CONGREGATION:** Sign *church* and then *group*.
**DEVIL, DEMON, SATAN:** Bend and unbend right index and middle fingers a few times. Right thumb touches temple.
**FAITHFUL:** Point both *F* hands forward with the right hand over the left. Move both hands forward while simultaneously strik-

ing the lower side of the right hand on the upper side of the left a few times.
**HOLY, DIVINE, HALLOWED, RIGHTEOUS, SANCTIFIED:** Make a right *H* hand; then move the right flat palm across the left flat palm from heel to fingertips. *Note:* Initialize each word individually.
**INCLUDE, INVOLVE:** Sweep the curved right open hand from right to left, and form the *and* hand before placing it in the left *C* hand.
**LAMB, SHEEP:** Open and close the right *V* fingers as they move up the left forearm. Add the sign for *small* when signing *lamb*.
**PASSOVER:** Tap the left elbow with the right *P* fingers a few times.

**SACRIFICE:** Place both *S* hands to the front with palms facing up, and move them in a forward-upward direction while simultaneously opening into palm-up flat hands.
**SPIRIT, GHOST:** Bring the right open hand down toward the left open hand with palms facing. Create *F* hands as the right hand is drawn upward.
**TITHE:** Sign *1* and then *10* a little lower.
**TRINITY:** Draw the right *3* hand down through the left *C* hand, and end with the right index pointing up.

LOOK IN INDEX FOR LOCATION OF ADDITIONAL DESCRIPTIONS.

and   Presbyterian   churches.   The   rabbi   joined

the priest   /   pastor   /   for   a   meeting.

/   innocent   /   bless   /   praise   /   glory   /   angel   /

/   anoint   /   heaven   /   religion   /   against   /   tempt   /

**AGAINST, OPPOSE:** Thrust the fingertips of the right flat hand into the palm of the left flat hand.

**ANGEL, WINGS:** Touch shoulders with fingertips of both hands, then swing them out and flap hands up and down a few times.

**ANOINT:** Tip C hand over top of head.

**BLESS:** Touch the lips with thumbs of both A hands, and move them forward to palm-down flat hands.

**GLORY, GLORIOUS:** Place the flat hands palm to palm, then raise the right hand while wiggling the fingers.

**HEAVEN, CELESTIAL:** Make a circle with both hands toward self; then pass the right hand under the left palm and up as the hands are crossed at forehead level.

**INNOCENT:** Touch the lips with both H fingers and move them forward and down with palms facing up.

**JOIN, ATTACH, UNITE:** Interlock the index fingers and thumbs of both hands with all other fingers extended.

**MEETING:** Bring both open hands in from the sides while forming and hands, and let the fingertips touch.

**PASTOR, PREACH, SERMON:** Move the right palm-forward F hand forward and backward a few times. For pastor, end with the sign for person (personalizing word ending).

**PRAISE, APPLAUD, CLAP:** Clap the

hands as many times as desired.

**PRESBYTERIAN:** Place (or tap) middle finger of P hand on left flat palm.

**PRIEST, CHAPLAIN, CLERGYMAN, MINISTER:** Draw the right Q fingertips backward around the right side of the neck.

**RABBI:** Place fingertips of both R hands on the chest and draw both hands down.

**RELIGION, RELIGIOUS:** Move the R fingers forward after touching the chest.

**TEMPT, ENTICE:** Tap the left elbow with the right bent index finger.

LOOK IN INDEX FOR LOCATION OF ADDITIONAL DESCRIPTIONS.

# Practice Giving Signs

Practice signing the following sentences once again. Try to do so without referring back to the illustrations. You can also cover the page opposite if you wish.

The missionary's ministry /vision/ was lost souls.

The Bible says love and forgive your neighbors.

The Lord brings truth /life/.

Moses sacrificed lambs at Passover.

The Trinity includes the Holy Spirit.

My congregation faithfully tithes.

The devil lies.

Our city has Baptists, Assemblies of God, and Presbyterian churches.

The rabbi joined the priest /pastor/ for a meeting.

/innocent/bless/praise/glory/angel/anoint/ heaven/religion/against/tempt/

# Vocabulary Review

Identify the following signs from this and previous chapters to reinforce your vocabulary.

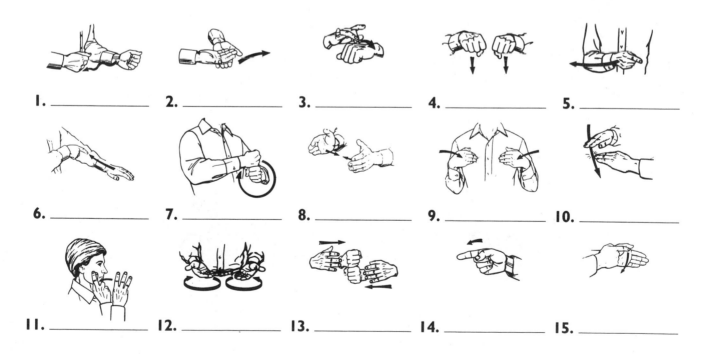

1. _____   2. _____   3. _____   4. _____   5. _____

6. _____   7. _____   8. _____   9. _____   10. _____

11. _____   12. _____   13. _____   14. _____   15. _____

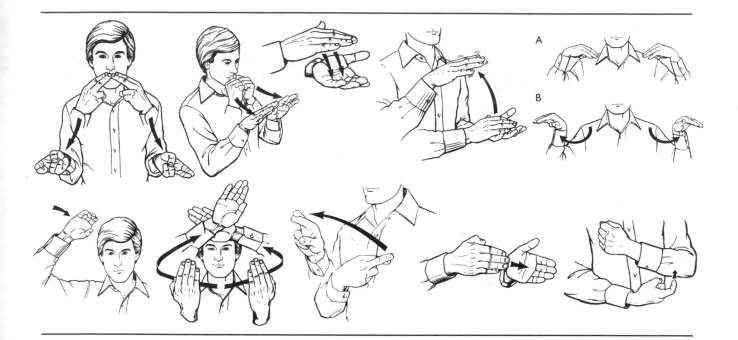

# Test Your Skill: Matching

This section uses standard matching techniques. See if you can match the signs with the words by writing the correct word next to the sign.

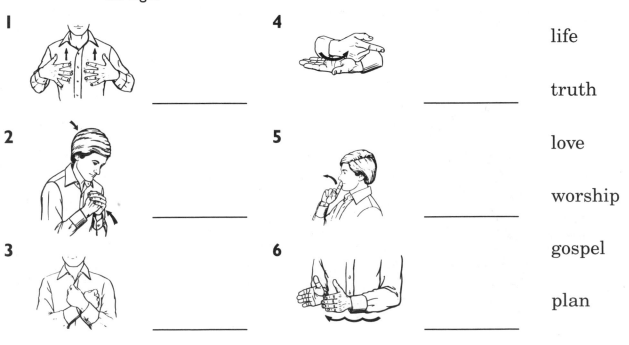

1 _____

2 _____

3 _____

4 _____

5 _____

6 _____

life

truth

love

worship

gospel

plan

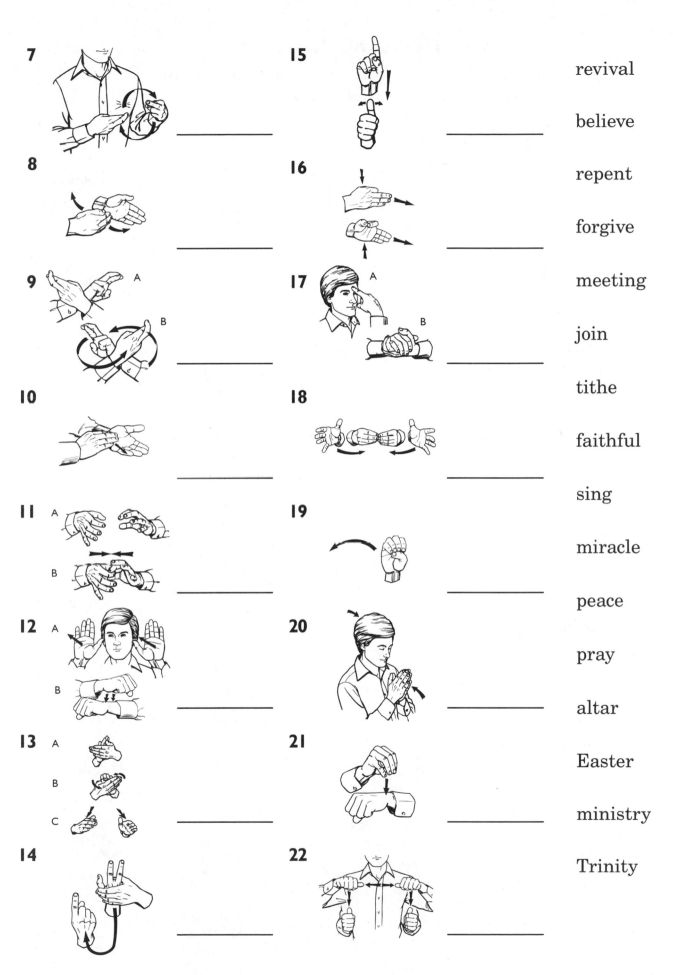

7 _____

8 _____

9 _____

10 _____

11 _____

12 _____

13 _____

14 _____

15 _____

16 _____

17 _____

18 _____

19 _____

20 _____

21 _____

22 _____

revival

believe

repent

forgive

meeting

join

tithe

faithful

sing

miracle

peace

pray

altar

Easter

ministry

Trinity

# Multiple Choice

Draw a circle around or place a check mark beside the sign that matches the italicized word. For additional practice you can sign all the words in the sentences.

**1** I worship at a *Baptist* church.

A    B    C

**2** She knelt at the altar to *meditate* and pray.

A    B    C

**3** We *celebrate* the resurrection of Jesus at Easter.

A    B    C

**4** They *welcomed* us to the sunrise service.

A    B    C

**5** The Bible tells us to *love* everyone.

A    B    C

**6** His missionary vision was *lost* souls.

A    B    C

**7** God gives everlasting *peace* to those who follow Him.

A    B    C

**8** She sang at the *church* meeting.

A    B    C

**9** We believe in *miracles*.

A    B    C

**10** You can *depend* on us for help.

A    B    C

**11** At *Passover* Moses sacrificed lambs.

A    B    C

**12** Do you ever wonder about *heaven*?

A    B    C

**13** Don't believe the devil's *lies*.

A    B    C

**14** The gospel is God's plan of love, grace, and *salvation*.

A    B    C

**15** Can you *accept* the truth of the Word?

A    B    C

**16** I am persuaded to follow *Jesus*.

A    B    C

# Vocabulary Review

Identify the following signs from this and previous chapters to reinforce your vocabulary.

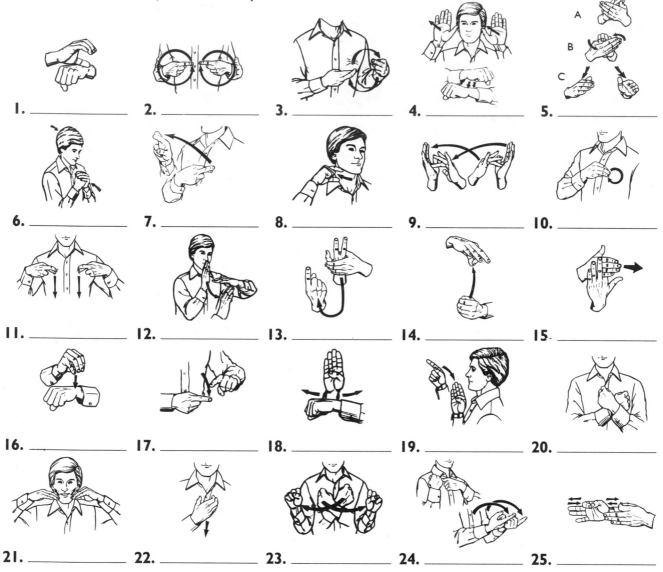

1. _____
2. _____
3. _____
4. _____
5. _____

6. _____
7. _____
8. _____
9. _____
10. _____

11. _____
12. _____
13. _____
14. _____
15. _____

16. _____
17. _____
18. _____
19. _____
20. _____

21. _____
22. _____
23. _____
24. _____
25. _____

# Extra Practice

Sign the following sentences which contain words chosen mainly from this chapter. This will give you additional practice using the signs you have just learned.

1 The Lord gives everlasting peace to those who repent.

2 Wonderful miracles happened often at the revival.

3 The minister spoke the truth to the people.

4 We celebrated communion at the Baptist church.

5 A congregation that faithfully tithes will be blessed.

6 The resurrection of Christ is a holy celebration at Easter.

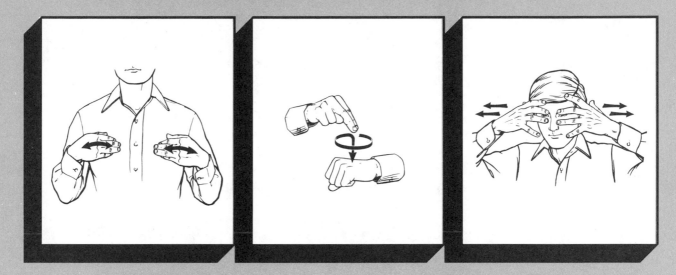

# Animals
# and
# Nature

## 12

# Practice Learning Signs

Learn and practice the signs and sentences on each page before proceeding to the next. Descriptions are supplied at the bottom of each page.

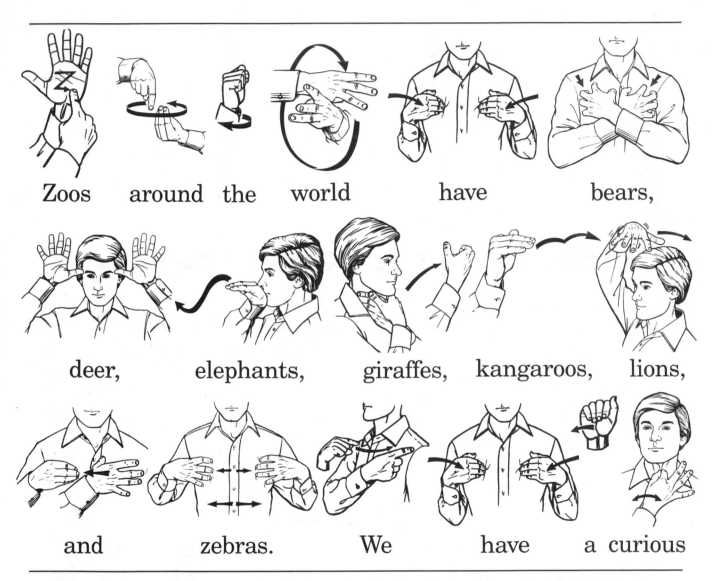

Zoos    around    the    world    have    bears,

deer,    elephants,    giraffes,    kangaroos,    lions,

and    zebras.    We    have    a curious

**AROUND, SURROUND:** Make a counterclockwise circle with the right index finger around the left upturned *and* hand.
**BEAR:** Cross the arms and claw at the chest a few times.
**CURIOUS, INQUISITIVE:** Pinch the skin in the front of the neck with the thumb and right index finger. Wiggle the hand from side to side.
**DEER, ANTLERS, MOOSE:** With palms facing forward, touch the temples with the thumbs of both open hands a few times. *Note: Moose* can be signed with the same movement but with the fingers closed rather than open.
**ELEPHANT:** Move the right curved hand

down from the mouth, and then forward and up. The fingertips lead the way throughout the movement.
**GIRAFFE:** Place the thumb and index finger of the left *C* hand on the neck. Touch the neck with the thumb and index finger of the right *C* hand, then move the right hand in a forward-upward direction. This sign can be made using only the right hand.
**KANGAROO:** Hold the right bent hand to the front with palm facing forward. Move the hand forward with several up-and-down movements. *Note:* This sign is sometimes done with two hands making identical movements.
**LION:** Shake the right curved open hand as

it moves backward over the head.
**WORLD:** Make a forward circle with the right *W* hand around the left *W* hand. End with the little-finger edge of the right *W* hand resting on the thumb side of the left *W* hand.
**ZEBRA:** Place both slightly curved open hands on the abdomen with palms touching the body. Draw both hands toward the sides and repeat the action on the body.
**ZOO:** Trace the letter *Z* on the left palm-front hand with the right index finger. *Note:* Some prefer to fingerspell.

LOOK IN INDEX FOR LOCATION OF ADDITIONAL DESCRIPTIONS.

male    cat,    a    female    dog,    and

horses.    Protect    the environment.    Squirrels    /    owls    /

live    in    trees.    Todd    likes

eagles,    foxes,    monkeys,    rabbits,    tigers,

**CAT:** Place the thumbs and index fingers of both *F* hands under the nose and move both hands out sideways. Some prefer to use only one hand.

**DOG:** Slap the thigh and snap the fingers.

**EAGLE:** Place the right *X* hand by the nose.

**ENVIRONMENT, CIRCUMSTANCE, SITUATION:** Circle the right *E* hand in a counterclockwise direction around the front of the left vertical index finger. Initialize with a *C* for *circumstance* and an *S* for *situation*.

**FEMALE:** Trace the right jawbone from ear to chin with the palm side of the right *A* thumb.

**FOX, SLY:** Place the *F*-hand circle over the nose and rotate the hand counterclockwise.

**HORSE:** Place extended *U*-hand thumb on temple. Bend and unbend *U* fingers.

**LIVE, ADDRESS, DWELL, RESIDE:** Move both *L* hands upward on the chest.

**MALE:** Grasp the bill of an imaginary cap and move the hand forward.

**MONKEY, APE:** Scratch the sides of the chest with both claw-shaped hands.

**OWL:** Look through both *O* hands and twist them toward the center and back a few times.

**PROTECT, DEFEND, GUARD:** With palms down, place the little-finger edge of the left *S* hand on the thumb side of the right *S* hand (or vice versa) and move hands forward.

**RABBIT:** Cross both *U* hands in front of the chest. Bend and unbend the *U* fingers.

**SQUIRREL, CHIPMUNK:** Tap fingertips of *V* hands against each other a few times.

**TIGER:** Move both open hands outward sideways from the face while changing them to claw-shaped hands.

**TREE, BRANCH, FOREST, WOODS:** Place the right elbow in the left palm. Pivot the right wrist and wiggle the fingers. Initialize for *branch, forest,* and *woods.*

LOOK IN INDEX FOR LOCATION OF ADDITIONAL DESCRIPTIONS.

turkeys, and turtles. Chickens, cows,

ducks, and goats were there

on the land. Look at all the wonderful

colors together: green grass, white

**ALL, ENTIRE, WHOLE:** Circle the right flat hand around the left flat hand. End with the back of the right hand in the palm of the left hand.

**CHICKEN:** Open and close the Q fingers at the mouth. Sometimes pecking at the left flat palm is added.

**COLOR:** Wiggle the fingers of the right open hand as the hand is moved forward from the mouth.

**COW:** Pivot both Y hands back and forth with the thumbs touching the temples.

**DUCK:** Open and close the N fingers and thumb in front of the mouth.

**GOAT:** Move the S hand up from the chin to a V hand with palm facing left.

**GRASS:** Sign green, then open the fingers of the right and hand as they pass up through the left C hand.

**GREEN:** Move the shaking G hand to the right.

**LAND, DIRT, FIELD, SOIL:** Rub the fingertips and thumbs of both and hands for dirt and soil. For land and field, add circles in opposite directions with both palm-down flat hands.

**LOOK AT, LOOK, OBSERVE, WATCH:** Point the right V fingers at the eyes and then in the direction desired.

**THERE:** Point in the appropriate direction.

**TOGETHER, ACCOMPANY:** Make a forward circle with both A hands.

**TURKEY:** Shake the Q hand in front of the chin while moving it down and forward.

**TURTLE:** Wiggle the A thumb from under the left curved hand.

**WHITE:** Move the curved open hand forward from the chest while changing to an and hand.

**WONDERFUL, GREAT, MARVELOUS:** Both flat hands move up and forward a few times.

LOOK IN INDEX FOR LOCATION OF ADDITIONAL DESCRIPTIONS.

clouds, blue sky, and flower

garden. The bug climbed between

the rocks. / animal / bird / plant / fly /

/ river / different / stubborn / restless /

**ANIMAL:** Put fingertips of both bent hands on the chest. Rock the hands sideways.

**BETWEEN:** Pivot the right flat hand back and forth between the thumb and index finger of the left flat hand.

**BIRD:** Open and close the *Q* fingers at the mouth.

**BLUE:** Move the right *B* hand to the right while shaking it from the wrist.

**BUG, INSECT:** Bend and unbend the 3-hand fingers with thumb touching nose.

**CLIMB, ASCEND:** Make alternate upward climbing movements with both curved *V*-finger hands.

**CLOUDS, STORM:** Move both curved open hands from side to side with circular movements.

**DIFFERENT, UNLIKE, VARIED:** Do an enlarged form of the sign for *but*.

**FLOWER:** Place the fingertips of the right *and* hand under each nostril separately.

**FLY (INSECT):** Imitate catching a fly on the left arm.

**GARDEN, YARD:** Move open hands in half-circles toward body; then sign *flower*.

**PLANT (VERB), SOW:** Imitate gradually dropping a handful of seeds by rubbing the thumb across the fingers as the hand moves to the right.

**RESTLESS:** Place the back of the right *V*

fingers in the left palm and pivot back and forth from the wrist.

**RIVER:** Sign *water;* then move both palm-down hands right with wiggling fingers.

**ROCK, STONE:** Strike the right closed hand on the back of the left closed hand; then hold both *C* hands slightly apart with palms facing.

**SKY, HEAVENS, SPACE:** Hold the right flat hand slightly above head level with the palm facing in. Move it in an arc from left to right. The hand may also be pivoted slightly from left to right during the movement.

**STUBBORN, DONKEY, OBSTINATE:** Bend the right hand at the temple.

LOOK IN INDEX FOR LOCATION OF ADDITIONAL DESCRIPTIONS.

# Practice Giving Signs

Practice signing the following sentences once again. Try to do so without referring back to the illustrations. You can also cover the page opposite if you wish.

Zoos around the world have bears, deer, elephants, giraffes, kangaroos, lions, and zebras.

We have a curious male cat, a female dog, and horses.

Protect the environment.

Squirrels /owls/ live in trees.

Todd likes eagles, foxes, monkeys, rabbits, tigers, turkeys, and turtles.

Chickens, cows, ducks, and goats were there on the land.

Look at all the wonderful colors together: green grass, white clouds, blue sky, and flower garden.

The bug climbed between the rocks.

# Fingerspelling Practice

Practice the following words at least twice with a speed that is both steady and comfortable for you.

| | | | | | |
|---|---|---|---|---|---|
| Bell | Edison | Pupin | Hammond | Morse | Alexanderson |
| De Forest | Augustine | St. Paul | Picasso | Einstein | Pasteur |
| Aristotle | Moses | Caesar | Wright | Bonaparte | Shakespeare |
| Planck | Monet | Homer | Plato | Beethoven | Fleming |
| Cromwell | Calvin | Bach | Bolívar | Locke | Morton |
| Van Gogh | Rockwell | Newton | Gutenburg | Columbus | Michelangelo |
| Urban | Harvey | Becquerel | Röntgen | Mendel | Rubens |

# Practice Receiving Signs

Interpret the following signs. Practicing by this method will help you receive and understand the signs more easily. Say the words out loud as you proceed.

# Test Your Skill: Matching

This section uses standard matching techniques. See if you can match the signs with the words by writing the correct word next to the sign.

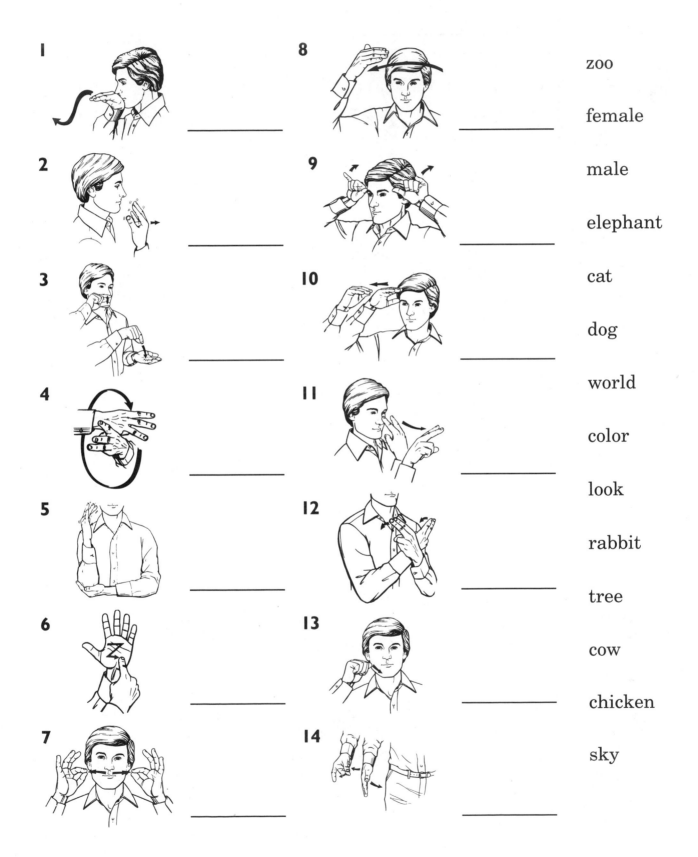

1 _____

2 _____

3 _____

4 _____

5 _____

6 _____

7 _____

8 _____

9 _____

10 _____

11 _____

12 _____

13 _____

14 _____

zoo

female

male

elephant

cat

dog

world

color

look

rabbit

tree

cow

chicken

sky

# Answers

## CHAPTER 1

*Vocabulary Review*   p. 35
1. parents;  2. mother;  3. fine;  4. kitchen;
5. name;  6. father;  7. please;  8. grandma;
9. where;  10. all right;  11. thanks;  12. husband;
13. wife.
*Multiple Choice*   p. 40
1.B;  2.A;  3.C;  4.A;  5.B.

## CHAPTER 2

*Multiple Choice*   p. 52
1.B;  2.C;  3.C;  4.A;  5.B;  6.A;  7.C;  8.B.
*Test Your Skill: Matching*   pp. 53–54
1. need;  2. idea;  3. late;  4. interest;  5. work;
6. boss;  7. give;  8. farm;  9. important;
10. schedule;  11. salary;  12. library;  13. imagination;  14. about;  15. control;  16. usually;
17. doctor;  18. machine;  19. announce;  20. advertise;  21. telephone;  22. cancel;  23. that;
24. problem.

## CHAPTER 3

*Test Your Skill: Matching*   p. 68
1. restaurant;  2. hamburger;  3. food;  4. supper;
5. cheese;  6. cake;  7. lunch,  8. drink;  9. hungry;
10. bread;  11. delicious;  12. candy;  13. water;
14. meat.

## CHAPTER 4

*Vocabulary Review*   p. 81
1. trip;  2. fly;  3. car;  4. gas;  5. Christmas;  6. lost;
7. suitcase;  8. vacation;  9. hotel;  10. street;
11. boat;  12. foreign;  13. hurry;  14. near;
15. camera.
*Multiple Choice*   pp. 84–85
1.A;  2.C;  3.C;  4.B;  5.A;  6.C;  7.B;  8.A;  9.C;
10.C;  11.B;  12.A.
*Test Your Skill: Matching*   pp. 86–87
1. travel;  2. car;  3. lost;  4. will;  5. street;  6. fly;
7. country;  8. traffic;  9. highway;  10. suitcase;
11. California;  12. Christmas;  13. vacation;
14. Canada;  15. Israel;  16. gas;  17. oil;  18. camera;  19. pictures;  20. park;  21. left;  22. boat;
23. west;  24. hotel;  25. Thanksgiving;  26. staying;  27. foreign;  28. south;  29. canoeing;
30. stamps.
*Fill In the Blanks*   p. 88   (possible answers)
1. (answers given);  2. next week, Israel;
3. camera, lost;  4. Canada, country;  5. trip, gas,
oil;  6. right, left;  7. north, Christmas;  8. picture,
friend;  9. traffic;  10. street;  11. hates, car, train;
12. international, weeks;  13. foreign, beautiful;
14. lost, traffic;  15. park;  16. continued, across;
17. street, live;  18. fun, canoeing;  19. visit,
soon;  20. here, go.

## CHAPTER 5

*Test Your Skill: Matching*   p. 100
1. skiing;  2. movie;  3. golf;  4. basketball;
5. game;  6. bicycling;  7. walking;  8. beat;

9. football;  10. skillful;  11. radio;  12. tennis;
13. practice;  14. group.
*Multiple Choice*   p. 101
1.C;  2.A;  3.A;  4.A;  5.B;  6.C;  7.B;  8.C.
*Vocabulary Review*   p. 102
1. at;  2. bowling;  3. smile;  4. were;  5. most;
6. taste;  7. was;  8. best;  9. work;  10. new;
11. coffee;  12. begin;  13. fine;  14. try;  15. need;
16. important;  17. late;  18. while;  19. toward;
20. on;  21. which;  22. smell;  23. next;
24. speech;  25. where.

## CHAPTER 6

*Vocabulary Review*   p. 115
1. past;  2. sun;  3. dark;  4. summer;  5. umbrella;
6. storm;  7. later;  8. cold;  9. spring;  10. future.
*Test Your Skill: Matching*   p. 116
1. ice;  2. winter;  3. slippery;  4. dry;  5. moon;
6. Friday;  7. until;  8. temperature;  9. warm;
10. tomorrow;  11. wait;  12. month;  13. hour;
14. forever.
*Multiple Choice*   pp. 117–118
1.B;  2.A;  3.C;  4.C;  5.A;  6.B;  7.B;  8.C;  9.A;
10.C;  11.C;  12.B;  13.B.

## CHAPTER 7

*Vocabulary Review*   p. 132
1. cute;  2. house;  3. hate;  4. spaghetti;  5. with;
6. this;  7. are;  8. love;  9. last;  10. drink;  11. wait;
12. happy;  13. explain;  14. much;  15. ask.
*Fill In the Blanks*   p. 136   (possible answers)
1. (answer given);  2. happy, positive;  3. proud,
honest;  4. patient;  5. exaggerates, experiences;
6. talk;  7. upset, friend's;  8. jealousy;  9. polite;
10. fear;  11. good, laugh;  12. awful, angered;
13. love, hate;  14. nervous;  15. successful;
16. thankful, demanding;  17. sorry, guilty;
18. awkward;  19. kind;  20. honest.

## CHAPTER 8

*Test Your Skill: Matching*   pp. 148–149
1. buy;  2. silver;  3. socks;  4. money;  5. profit;
6. loan;  7. shirt;  8. store;  9. worthless;  10. borrow;  11. expensive;  12. hat;  13. cost;  14. save;
15. skirt;  16. sign (signature);  17. owe;
18. cheap;  19. decide;  20. mistake;  21. pay;
22. dollars;  23. shoes;  24. subtract;  25. compare;  26. steal;  27. sell;  28. count;  29. list;
30. collect.
*Multiple Choice*   p. 150
1.C;  2.B;  3.B;  4.A;  5.C.

## CHAPTER 9

*Vocabulary Review*   p. 163
1. psychology;  2. teach;  3. understand;  4. mind;
5. lipreading;  6. lesson;  7. school;  8. attention;
9. discuss;  10. junior.
*Test Your Skill: Matching*   p. 164
1. paragraph;  2. smart;  3. philosophy;  4. measure;  5. difficult;  6. ignorant;  7. learn;  8. fingerspelling;  9. senior;  10. write;  11. graduate;

12. dictionary;  13. inform;  14. broad-minded.
*Multiple Choice*   pp. 165–166
1.B;  2.C;  3.C;  4.B;  5.A;  6.B;  7.C;  8.A;  9.C;
10.A;  11.B;  12.B;  13.C.

## CHAPTER 10

*Vocabulary Review*   p. 179
1. than;  2. from;  3. bad;  4. fail;  5. do;  6. later;
7. receive;  8. will;  9. every;  10. complain;
11. much;  12. won't;  13. wait;  14. through;
15. soon.
*Test Your Skill: Matching*   pp. 182–184
1. body;  2. good;  3. healthy;  4. doctor;  5. habit;
6. exercise;  7. accident;  8. gave;  9. medicine;
10. smoking;  11. nurse;  12. danger;  13. blame;
14. mumps;  15. head.  16. toilet;  17. pain;  18. injection;  19. help;  20. nervous;  21. operation;
22. death;  23. poison;  24. X ray;  25. rescue;
26. pregnant;  27. tired;  28. shock;  29. suffer;
30. weak;  31. sick;  32. hospital;  33. fire;
34. cough;  35. police;  36. audiology;  37. broken;  38. cold.
*Multiple Choice*   p. 185
1.A;  2.C;  3.A;  4.C;  5.B;  6.C;  7.A;  8.B.
*Fill In the Blanks*   p. 186   (possible answers)
1. (answers given);  2. shock, death;  3. hospital,
broken;  4. medicine, pain;  5. healthy, body;
6. cigarettes;  7. police, drowning;  8. earthquake;  9. killed, flood;  10. escaped, destructive;
11. arm, operation;  12. haircut, Saturday;
13. blame;  14. dentist;  15. tired, lie down;
16. cold, cough;  17. nurse, injection;  18. fire,
damage;  19. exercise;  20. escaped.

## CHAPTER 11

*Vocabulary Review*   p. 199
1. avoid;  2. birth;  3. early;  4. can;  5. them;
6. long;  7. year;  8. small;  9. has;  10. than;
11. were;  12. here;  13. get;  14. there;
15. what.
*Test Your Skill: Matching*   pp. 202–203
1. life;  2. worship;  3. love;  4. gospel;  5. truth;
6. plan;  7. revival;  8. sing;  9. repent;  10. forgive;
11. join;  12. miracle;  13. peace;  14. Trinity;
15. tithe;  16. faithful;  17. believe;  18. meeting;
19. Easter;  20. pray;  21. ministry;  22. altar.
*Multiple Choice*   pp. 204–205
1.A;  2.C;  3.C;  4.A;  5.C;  6.B;  7.B;  8.B;  9.A;
10.B;  11.A;  12.C;  13.B;  14.C;  15.B;  16.C.
*Vocabulary Review*   p. 206
1. church;  2. sin;  3. revival;  4. miracle;  5. peace;
6. worship;  7. religion;  8. priest;  9. Jesus;
10. missionary;  11. rabbi;  12. humble;  13. Trinity;  14. soul;  15. through;  16. ministry;  17. cannot;  18. busy;  19. God;  20. love;  21. smile;
22. wish;  23. salvation;  24. since;  25. explain.

## CHAPTER 12

*Test Your Skill: Matching*   p. 216
1. elephant;  2. color;  3. chicken;  4. world;
5. tree;  6. zoo;  7. cat;  8. sky;  9. cow;  10. male;
11. look;  12. rabbit;  13. female;  14. dog.

# Additional Descriptions

**ABOVE (COMPARATIVE DEGREE), EXCEED, MORE THAN, OVER:** Hold both bent hands to the front of the body with the right fingers on top of the left fingers. Raise the bent right hand a short distance.

**ACCURATE, EXACT, PRECISE, SPECIFIC:** Place the thumb tips and index fingertips of each hand together. Position the right hand with palm facing forward and the left hand with palm facing the right hand. Move the hands together until the thumb and index fingers touch.

**AND:** Place the right open hand in front with palm facing in and fingers pointing to the left. Move the hand to the right while bringing the fingertips and thumb together.

**ANY, ANYBODY, ANYONE:** Place the right *A* hand in front of the body with the palm facing in. Move the *A* hand forward to the right until the palm faces forward. Add the numerical sign for *one* when signing *anyone* and *anybody*. *One* is signed by pointing up with the right index finger.

**ASSEMBLIES OF GOD:** Put thumb of right *A* hand on forehead; then point right *G* finger forward and upward at head level. (Some use the flat hand with palm facing left.) Move right hand in a downward arc toward self, ending with a *B* hand in front of the chest. The second part is the sign for *God*.

**ATTENTION, CONCENTRATION, FOCUS, PAY ATTENTION:** Hold both flat hands at the sides of the face with palms facing; then move them both forward simultaneously.

**AUDIOLOGY:** Circle the right *A* hand in a clockwise direction at the right ear.

**BED:** Hold both hands palm to palm and place the back of the left hand on the right cheek. *Alternative* (not illustrated): Place the slightly curved right hand on the right cheek and tilt the head to the right.

**BELOW (COMPARATIVE DEGREE), LESS THAN, UNDER:** Hold both bent hands to the front with the left fingers on top of the right fingers. Lower the right hand a short distance.

**BLANKET:** Hold both open hands to the front with palms facing down and fingers pointing down. Lift both hands to shoulder level while closing the thumbs on the index fingers.

**BOAST, BRAG, SHOW OFF:** Move one or both *A*-hand thumbs in and out at the sides just above the waist.

**BOWLING:** Swing the right curved hand forward from behind the body to the front.

**BREAK, FRACTURE, SNAP:** Hold the thumb and index-finger sides of both *S* hands together; then twist them both sharply outward and apart.

**BREAST:** Place the fingertips of the right curved hand at the left breast and then at the right.

**CAMERA:** Hold both hands with the thumbs and bent index fingers in front of the face. Keep the other fingers closed. Raise and lower the right index finger.

**CANCEL, ANNUL, CORRECT, CRITICIZE:** Trace an *X* on the left palm with the right index finger.

**CHOOSE, PICK, SELECT:** Use the right thumb and index finger to make a picking motion from the front as the hand is drawn back toward self. The remaining right fingers are extended. Sometimes the fingers of the left hand are held up in front of the right, and the right appears to be deciding which finger to choose.

**CLOSE, SHUT:** Bring both flat hands together from the sides with palms facing forward.

**COMFORT:** Rub the right curved hand over the back of the left, and vice versa.

**CONFESS, ACKNOWLEDGE, ADMIT:** Begin with the fingertips of both hands pointing down and touching the chest. Simultaneously move the hands in an upward-forward arc until they are pointing forward with palms facing up.

**DIRTY, FILTHY, FOUL, NASTY:** Place the back of the right hand under the chin and wiggle the fingers.

**DOWN:** Point the right index finger down with palm facing in, and move it down slightly.

**DRUNK, INTOXICATE:** Move the thumb of the right *A* (or *Y*) hand backward and downward toward the mouth.

**DRY, DROUGHT, PARCHED:** Move right curved index finger across the lips from left to right.

**EAGER, AMBITIOUS, ANXIOUS, EARNEST, ENTHUSIASTIC, ZEAL:** Rub the flat hands together enthusiastically.

**EAR, HEAR, NOISE, SOUND:** Touch or point to the right ear with the right index finger.

**EASTER:** Move the right *E* hand in a sideways arc to the right with the palm facing

forward.

**FARM, COUNTRY:** Bend the left arm and rub the left elbow with the right flat hand.

**FOLLOW, DISCIPLE, SEQUEL, CHASE, PURSUE:** Place both *A* hands to the front with the left one slightly ahead of the right. Move them forward with the right hand following the left. *Note:* Add the sign for *person* (personalizing word ending) when signing *follower, disciple* (can be initialized), or *chaser. Chase* and *pursue* are signed more rapidly than *follow*.

**FOREIGN:** Rub the index finger and thumb side of the right *F* hand in a few counterclockwise circles on the underside of the left forearm near the elbow.

**FRIDAY:** Make a small clockwise circle with the right *F* hand.

**GET, ACQUIRE, OBTAIN, RECEIVE:** Bring both open hands together while simultaneously forming *S* hands and place the right on top of the left. The hands can be moved toward the body, especially when signing *receive*.

**GET OUT, GET IN, GET OFF:** Hold right *V* fingers in left *O* and pull them out. Reverse the action to sign *get in*.

**GONE, ABSENT:** Draw the right open hand down through the left *C* hand and end with the right hand in the *and* position below the left hand.

**GUESS, MISS (LET SLIP OR LET GO):** The same basic sign is used for both words. Move the right *C* hand across the face from right to left and close to a downturned *S* position.

**HAT:** Pat the top of the head with the right flat hand.

**HE, HIM:** First sign *male;* then point the index finger forward. If it is obvious that a male is being referred to, the sign for *male* can be omitted.

**HEART (EMOTIONAL):** Outline the shape of a heart on the chest with both index or middle fingers.

**HI, HELLO:** Move the right *B* hand to the right from a position by the right temple.

**IGNORANT:** Place the back of the right *V* hand on the forehead. It can tap the forehead a few times if emphasis is required.

**KITCHEN:** Place the right *K* hand first palm down, then palm up on the upturned left palm.

**LATE, BEHIND TIME, NOT YET, NOT DONE, TARDY:** Let the right hand hang loosely in the area between armpit and waist. Move the hand back and forth from the wrist several times.

**LEFT (DIRECTION):** Move the right *L* hand toward the left.

**LIE, FALSEHOOD:** Point the right index finger to the left and move it horizontally across the lips from right to left.

**LIST:** Place the little-finger edge of the bent right hand on the fingers of the left flat hand. Move the right hand down the left hand in several short arcs.

**LONELY, LONESOME:** Hold the right index finger in front of the lips with the palm facing left. Move the index finger down across the lips a few times.

**LONG:** Extend the left flat hand to the front with palm facing down. Run the right index finger up the left arm, beginning at the fingertips.

**MEET, ENCOUNTER:** Bring both *D* hands together from the sides with palms facing.

**MENSTRUATION, PERIOD:** Tap the right cheek twice with the palm side of the right *A* hand.

**MOON:** Hold the shape of the right *C* hand around the right eye.

**MY, MINE, OWN, PERSONAL:** Place the palm of the right flat hand on the chest.

**NAPKIN:** Wipe the fingertips of the right flat hand across the lips.

**NIGHT, ALL NIGHT:** Hold the left arm in a horizontal position with the fingers of the left downturned flat hand pointing right. Place the right forearm on the back of the left hand and point the right curved hand downward. To sign *all night,* make a downward sweeping motion from right to left with the right hand.

**OPEN:** Place the thumbs and index fingers of both flat hands together with the palms facing forward. (Some prefer the palms facing down.) Move both hands sideways in opposite directions.

**PEPPER:** Hold the right *O* hand to the front with the *O* pointing down to the left. Shake down to the left a few times.

**PLATE:** Make a circle with the thumbs and fingers of both hands.

**PRAY, PRAYER:** Place both flat hands to the front with palms touching; then move them toward self while simultaneously inclining the head slightly forward.

**RED:** Stroke the lips downward with the right index finger (or *R* fingers).

**RESPECT:** Move the right *R* hand in a backward arc toward the face. The head is often bowed simultaneously.

**REST, RELAX, UNWIND:** Fold the arms in a natural position. Sometimes the *R* hands are used. *Alternative* (not illustrated): Cross the flat (or *R*) hands over the chest.

**REVENGE:** Position the fingertips of the index fingers and thumbs of both hands together, with the other fingers closed and palms facing each other. Strike the index fingers and thumbs together a few times.

**RIGHT (DIRECTION):** Move the right *R* hand toward the right.

**RUN, SPRINT:** Place both flat hands palm to palm with the right hand under the left. Slide the right hand quickly forward. *Alternative:* Point both *L* hands forward and hook the right index finger around the left thumb. Wiggle the thumbs and index fingers as both hands move forward quickly.

**SATURDAY:** Make a small clockwise circle with the right *S* hand.

**SECRET, CONFIDENTIAL, PERSONAL, PRIVATE:** Place the right *A* thumb over the pursed lips a few times. In addition, the *A* thumb is sometimes moved down under the palm of the curved left hand.

**SEEM, APPARENT, APPEAR:** Hold the curved right hand up with palm facing left. Turn the hand from the wrist so that the palm faces the head. The signer often glances at the hand to emphasize the meaning.

**SINCE, ALL ALONG, SO FAR:** Place both index-finger hands before the right shoulder with palms facing in, and index fingers pointing toward the shoulder. Bring both hands down and forward simultaneously until the index fingers are pointing forward with the palms facing up.

**SMELL, FRAGRANCE, FUMES, ODOR, SCENT:** Pass the slightly curved palm of the right hand upward in front of the nose a few times.

**SOMETIMES, OCCASIONALLY, ONCE IN A WHILE, SELDOM:** Hold the left flat hand at chest level with palm facing right. Touch the left palm with the right index fingertip; then move the right index finger upward to a vertical position. Repeat after a slight pause.

**SWEET:** Brush the right fingertips downward over the lips. Sometimes this is done on the chin.

**SWIMMING:** Place the slightly curved hands to the front with the backs of the hands partially facing each other and the fingers pointing forward. Move the hands simultaneously forward and to the sides.

**THROW, TOSS:** Place the right *A* hand beside the right side of the head. Move the right hand quickly forward while simultaneously opening it.

**TOILET, BATHROOM, RESTROOM:** Shake the right *T* hand in front of the chest with the palm facing forward. *Restroom* can also be signed by pointing the right *R* hand forward and moving it in a short arc to the right.

**TUESDAY:** Make a small clockwise circle with the right *T* hand.

**UMBRELLA:** Hold the right closed hand over the left closed hand; then raise the right hand a short distance.

**UP:** Hold up the right index finger with palm facing forward and move it up slightly. This word is sometimes fingerspelled.

**USE, USEFUL, UTILIZE:** With the palm facing forward, make a clockwise circle with the right *U* hand.

**VANILLA:** Shake the right *V* hand.

**VOLLEYBALL:** Hold both flat hands at head level with palms facing forward. Move them forward and upward.

**VOLUNTEER, APPLY, CANDIDATE:** Take a piece of clothing near the right shoulder between the thumb and index finger of the right hand, and pull it away from the body a few times. If a jacket or suit is worn, the lapel may be used.

**WARN, CAUTION:** Pat the back of the left flat hand with the right flat hand a few times.

**WASH DISHES, DISHWASHING:** With palms facing, rub the right flat hand in a clockwise circle over the left flat hand.

**WEDNESDAY:** Make a small clockwise circle with the right *W* hand.

**WIDE, BROAD:** Place both flat hands to the front with palms facing and draw them apart to the sides.

**WRESTLING, WRESTLER:** Interlock the fingers of both hands and move them back and forth in front of the chest. To sign *wrestler,* add *person* (personalizing word ending).

**YOU:** Point the right index finger to the person being addressed. Or, if referring to several people, make a sweeping motion from left to right.

# Index

The index that follows contains a complete listing of the words included in *Signing Made Easy*. Many signs have several synonyms in English. The main entries, in boldface in the index, refer readers to the page on which they will find the first occurrence of a sign in the book and a description of how to make that sign. Entries that are not in boldface are synonyms; to find the page that contains the description of how to make the sign, look under the appropriate main entry. A few main entries are followed by more than one page reference. Whenever this occurs, the first page number refers to the page on which the sign first appears; the second refers to the list of additional sign descriptions on pages 218–219.

224